The Furness Railway

in and around
Barrow

Michael Andrews

CUMBRIAN
RAILWAYS
ASSOCIATION

Front Cover

Top
The Furness Railway crest, based on the seal of Furness Abbey.

Middle left
General Offices, Barrow, c.1905. (Geoff Holme collection)

Middle right
Lady Moyra *at Ramsden Dock Station, c.1910. (Phil Cousins collection)*

Bottom
The 1.35pm Barrow to Crewe, c.1960. Jubilee No. 45568 Western Australia *in immaculate condition is on a 'running in' turn from major overhaul at Crewe works. It has one of the ten high-flatsided tenders built prior to the introduction of the Stanier tender. (Ken Norman)*

Text © M Andrews and the Cumbrian Railways Association 2003
Maps © M Andrews/ A Johnstone and the Cumbrian Railways Association 2003
Photographs © as credited

**Published by the Cumbrian Railways Association,
104 Durley Avenue, Pinner, Middlesex HA5 1JH
The Association is a Registered Charity No. 1025436
www.cumbrian-rail.org**

Membership Secretary, 36 Clevelands Avenue, Barrow-in-Furness, Cumbria. LA13 0AE

Design and layout by Alan Johnstone,
24 Hartington Street, Barrow-in-Furness, Cumbria. LA14 5SL
Printed by Lambert Print & Design, Settle, North Yorkshire

ISBN 0-9540232-1-8

Salthouse Junction, 15th July 1967. Signalman David Evans, Tim Andrews and the signal box cat. Boxes were always kept in immaculate condition, and, to stop the levers tarnishing, the signalman would use a cloth when operating the levers. (Author MAA16)

In memory of Tim Andrews
B.Eng., C.Eng., M.I.Mech.E., 1963-2001

Barrow Central, 21st October 1953. Unnamed Patriot 45513 of Carlisle Upperby (12A) stands with the Barrow - Preston coach at the south end of Platform 3 waiting to take the 9 am London express forward. At the north end of the platform, the station pilot waits to place the Barrow - London coach onto the rear of the Workington - London Euston through portion. The author's father, Jack Andrews, poses with the engine crew.
(Author MAC 91)

CONTENTS

INTRODUCTION

Within the local history literature of Furness, a book on the role of the Furness Railway Company in the development of the town of Barrow-in-Furness is long overdue. While this book is not a definitive history of either the town of Barrow or of the Furness Railway, it attempts to show how the railway influenced the development of the town and its industrial base from earliest days when it carried iron ore from Dalton and slate from Kirkby for shipment at Barrow harbour.

The Furness Railway directors were instrumental in the development of Barrow's main industries, being active in the Iron and Steelworks, Jute works and Shipyard. They also provided the land for other entrepreneurs to set up their own supporting enterprises, most of which brought additional traffic to the railway. When in 1897 their Barrow Shipyard was purchased by Vickers it was the latter company which dictated the pace of Barrow's development.

This book started life 49 years ago when the author enrolled in a London University night-school course in Railway History Studies. The students were required to research and write a dissertation on a railway history subject of their choice. Introductions were given to the Public Record Office, the House of Lords Record Office, the British Library and the British Transport Historical Records. Material in these institutions allowed an in-depth study of Barrow's railway system, a subject never tackled before, and on completion a copy of the dissertation was lodged in Barrow Reference Library. This was read some five years ago by Geoff Holme of Barrow who suggested to the author that the dissertation could be brought up to the present day, illustrated and published. Hard work by a small team has resulted in the book now being placed before the public.

St Luke's Junction, 1958. Britannia No. 70046 later named Anzac *pilots the 1.00pm express from Barrow to London Euston. (Author MAA 56)*

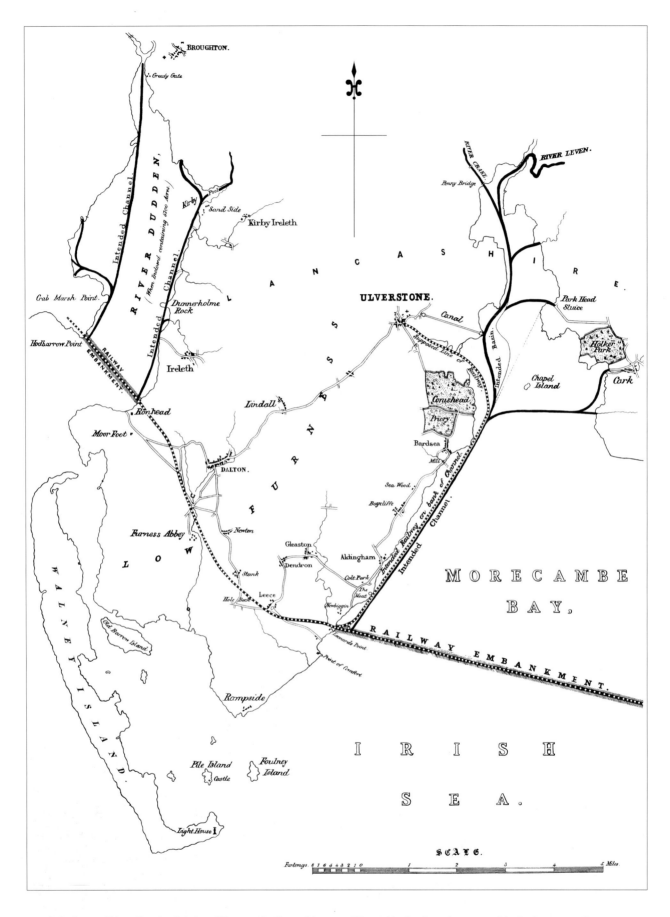

Caledonian, West Cumberland and Furness Railway. *Hague and Rastrick's plan from the report of the Parliamentary Committee on railway routes between London and Glasgow, 19th May 1840. Note the proposed branch railway to Ulverston and the channel for the Ulverston Canal.*
(Geoff Holme Collection)

The Borough of Barrow-in-Furness occupies the south-western tip of the Furness peninsula. To the north lies the estuary of the Duddon River, to the south Morecambe Bay, and, to the west, the islands of Walney and Barrow shelter the town from the Irish Sea. Between the south end of Walney Island and the coast lie three small islands, Roa, Piel and Foulney, forming a natural harbour used by ships as a refuge from westerly gales since medieval times.

To the north are two areas of high ground separated by a steep sided valley, where once a great river draining the Duddon Glacier ran, and which now contains a stream known as the Abbey Beck. The coastal plain, with the exception of the sand dunes on the west coast at Sandscale, consists of alluvial clay. The rock is New Red Sandstone in the south-west but, to the north and east, iron ore bearing Carboniferous Limestone extends into the Borough. It was the extraction of this ore which led to the rapid industrial development of the area during the nineteenth century.

In 1830 Dalton was the only town of any size in south-west Furness, and the Barrow district was included in the Parish of Dalton. There were numerous small hamlets occupied by farmers, many owning iron ore carts in which the ore was carried from the mines at Whitriggs near Lindal to the coast. Iron ore had been mined on a small scale in Furness for centuries and although, during the Napoleonic Wars, the export of iron ore had fallen off considerably, by 1830 it was rising again. The channel between Barrow Island and the mainland provided a natural harbour where ore boats could be brought up onto the beach at high tide, and at low tide they could be loaded with ore from the carts. The hamlet of Barrow, situated as it was within this harbour, had become the most important loading point on this part of the coast.

From the northern entrance of Barrow Channel the coastline ran due north past the hamlets of Cocken and Ormsgill, with the village of Hawcoat away to the east on the top of a hill. From the south end of the Channel the coast was marshy, and passed eastwards to the mouth of the Abbey Beck. This area was named Salthouse Marsh after the nearby hamlet, and has now been entirely covered by the building of streets, factories and docks. From Salthouse the coast ran south-east to Westfield Point and then on to Rampside where it turned north-east along the shore of Morecambe Bay.

As early as 1782 the Newland Company of ore miners and shippers built a jetty at Barrow to enable ore to be loaded into ships more quickly. This was followed, in 1832, by a second jetty, that of Messrs Town & Rawlinson, and, in 1839, a third built by Messrs Kennedy. The export of ore was, however, limited by the available means of transport. The road had been improved by the ironmasters but it gave only very limited facilities; three trips a day being the most that could be done by one cart, it was not surprising that alternative means of transport were considered. As early as 1825, a survey was made with the idea of building a tramway from the mines to Barrow, but these were early

Lancaster Sands by J M W Turner RA. Engraved 1828. Until the opening of the Ulverstone & Lancaster Railway in 1857 the short route between 'mainland' Lancashire and Furness & Cartmel was 'oversands'. The Duchy of Lancaster provided guides. The hazards and discomfort of the crossing are well shown.   *(Authors collection)*

7

days in railway development and the scheme came to nothing. In 1842 Job Bintley, a Civil Engineer of Kendal, made a more thorough survey and proposed two routes from Dalton to Barrow. The first ran through the valley northwards from Dalton to Park, then followed the coast westwards before turning south to Ormsgill. The second followed the Abbey Beck to Furness Abbey before turning west to Barrow via Newbarns.

Around this time, local attention was focused on much grander railway schemes. In 1837 the Whitehaven, Workington & Maryport Railway Committee asked George Stephenson to survey, and give an estimate for, a trunk route to Scotland via the West Coast, involving the crossing of Morecambe Bay and the Duddon Estuary. His route passed north of Barrow through a tunnel under Kirkby Moor. The scheme proved too expensive to those interested, so in 1838 a second major scheme was put forward by John Rastrick and John Hague (see map on page 6). Hague produced a plan for *cheap crossings* of the two stretches of water, and Rastrick planned the line of railway over land. The *Morecambe Bay Embankment* 11 miles long from Poulton (now known as Morecambe) was to have reached Furness just north of the present Borough boundary at Leonard's Point. A branch to Ulverston would have left the main line here. Then the main line would have passed northwards across the coastal plain, tunnelled under Yarlside Hill, and then followed the Abbey Beck,

avoiding the curve in the valley near the Abbey ruins by a deep cutting. From the north end of this cutting it was to run north-west through the Goldmire Valley to Park and the Duddon, crossing this on a second embankment. The line was to have risen at 1 in 330 to the summit at Yarlside, and then fall at the same gradient.

Local landowners, visualising the opening up of the district, backed the scheme, with Gale and Kennedy of Ulverston, Fell of Spark Bridge and Alcock Beck of Hawkshead being among the more active supporters. Had the scheme been adopted the development of Barrow would have been very different and probably on a much smaller scale. It would have featured, not as a terminus and point of export, but as a wayside halt on a trunk route. This *West Coast Scheme* of the Caledonian, West Cumberland and Furness Railway had however a serious rival, the proposed Lancaster to Penrith and Carlisle line. Independent observers criticised the West Cumberland route; *Investigator*, writing in the *Railway Magazine* of 1839, re-estimated the cost of the planned embankment at £1,847,360, whereas Hague's figure had been £434,131. Although the Cumberland Coast Scheme involved the reclaiming of a large area of land from the sea, a Parliamentary Committee of Investigation decided in favour of the overland route subsequently taken by the Lancaster and Carlisle Railway.

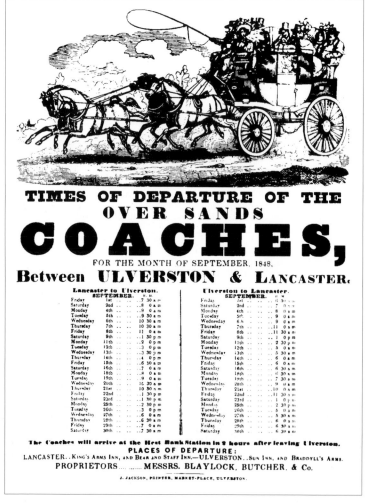

Oversands coach timetable for 1848. The times varied with the tides.

The most important step towards the creation of a railway in the Barrow district was the result of a survey carried out by the eminent engineer James Walker. His main object was to plan an embanking scheme for the Duddon Sands, but he also surveyed a local mineral line in Furness. On the abandonment of the Duddon Sands scheme the local survey was examined by the two principal landowners, the Earl of Burlington, later Duke of Devonshire, and the Duke of Buccleuch, who agreed to support it. J R Wright on behalf of Messrs Walker and Burgess, Engineers and Surveyors, then carried out a more detailed survey in 1843. A book of reference of land owners, lease holders and occupiers was compiled and a prospectus issued by the promoters, a group of London businessmen led by Benjamin Currey, Auditor of the Devonshire Estates.

The prospectus called attention to *the inadequacy of the present means of transit* and to the fact that this lack of rapid and cheap transport largely excluded the high quality ore and slate extracted in Furness from markets outside the area. It also took care to mention the fact that Buccleuch and Burlington were backing the project. The line was planned for working by horse power, but investors were assured that it was so designed that changeover to locomotive traction would be easily and cheaply accomplished should that become practical or necessary. The cost of the line was estimated at £100,000,

and the table assessing returns was based on hopes rather than facts. The forecast tonnage of ore was 100,000 tons per annum and the charge was to be 1s 6d (7.5p) per ton, but at that time the export of ore was of the order of 40,000 tons per annum only. The percentage of takings to be set aside for working expenses was put at 25% (when railways had become well established, 50% was considered a creditable figure), and in fact the estimated dividend of 8% was not reached until 10 years after the opening of the line.

There were to be two loading termini: Kirkby, where Lord Burlington had built a short railway in 1840 to carry slate for shipment at Kirkby Pool, and Ulverston. Because of opposition in the latter town the terminus was brought westwards to Lindal. The Kirkby Branch was to cross the pre-1974 Borough boundary at Thwaite Flat and then pass through the Goldmire valley to join the line from Lindal at Little Mill just south of Dalton. From here it was to follow the winding valley of the Abbey Beck, crossing the Barrow-Dalton road on the level at Little Mill and pass through the ruins of Furness Abbey on a curve of 15 chains radius. From Little Mill the gradient was to fall steeply at about 1 in 80 to Furness Abbey and to flatten out gradually to level at Roose. At Roose two roads were to be crossed and the line was then to divide into the Piel and Barrow Branches, these two termini being described as the two points most suitable for the loading of shipping.

Piel Station on Roa Island, c. 1910. The branch train from Barrow Central has just arrived, hauled by FR 2-4-0 No 46. Piel Station, Piel Pier and the embankment to Rampside were owned by John Abel Smith, a Preston & Wyre Railway shareholder. He sold out to the Furness Railway in 1853. The photograph was taken from the top of the Watch Tower which still survives. The station building shown dates from about 1868. In the left background is the embankment which led to Piel Pier.   *(Lawrence Allen collection)*

The line to Rampside was to curve away from the main line at Roose, cross the Barrow-Roosecote Road on the level, proceed along the shore and then cross Westfield Point to Rampside where Smith was building an inn near Conkle Hole. The Barrow Branch was to cross the Barrow-Rampside road on the level at Salthouse, then cross the sand on the Barrow Embankment, which curved round Rabbit Hill Point and ran along the shore to Barrow village, where it was to pass through the iron ore yards, ending in the most northerly yard.

Most landowners and occupiers were in favour of the proposed line, but there was some opposition at Barrow as well as Ulverston. William Fisher owned a large lime kiln and farm at Barrow through which the railway was to pass, and he opposed the line. The Kirkby Ireleth and Kirkby Kendal Turnpike Trustees, foreseeing future competition were also against the scheme, and their opposition was reflected in the FR Act of 1844. This contained a clause obliging the FR Co. to screen their line from the Ulverston Turnpike Road if the Trustees should find that their horses were frightened by the sight of the locomotive engines. With this clause inserted (later embraced by the Railway Clauses Consolidation Act 1844), the FR bill is recorded as unopposed. Those in favour of the line included Henry

William Cavendish, 7th Duke of Devonshire & 2nd Earl of Burlington, 1808-1891. He was chairman of the Furness Railway Company, 1848 - 1888, and a major investor in Barrow industry. (From Mackereths Furness Directory 1899, Geoff Holme collection)

The promoters were forced to project two lines to the coast, as, although ore was at this time shipped almost entirely from Barrow, John Abel Smith, a London banker, who had bought Roa Island for £500, proposed to build a pier and a causeway to the mainland at Rampside, the Act of Parliament for which had received Royal Assent on the 27th June 1843. Piel Harbour had the advantage over Barrow Harbour of allowing fixed sailing times uninfluenced by the tide, and it was Smith's intention to run a steamer service in connection with the Preston and Wyre Railway at Fleetwood, which he hoped would eventually become the main passenger route to Scotland. He also hoped that Piel would become the export point for Furness minerals, and so the Furness Railway promoters could not afford to neglect Piel and Smith.

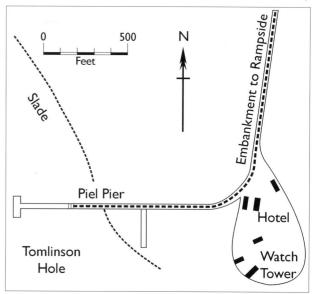

Roa Island, c.1847. First edition Ordnance survey.

Piel Pier, an artist's impression, c.1850. While the height of the hills in the background has been exaggerated, the three levels of the original pier opened in 1846 are shown. No photographs of the original pier or its 1868 replacement have been found. (Cumbria Record Office & Local Studies Library, Barrow BDSo/4/14/57)

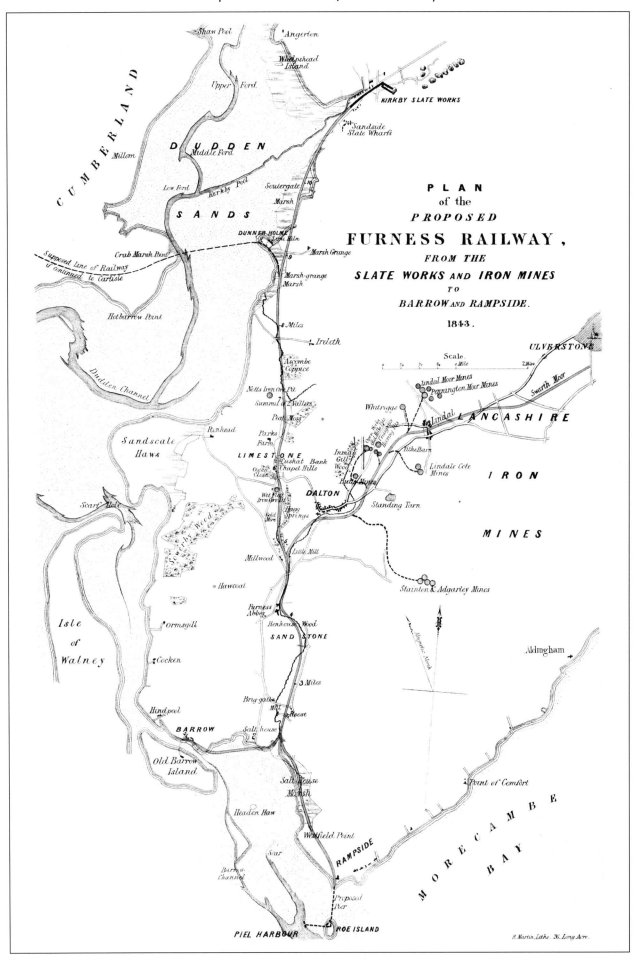

James Walker's plan of 1843

(Cumbria Record Office & Local Studies Library, Barrow ZK 45)

Schneider, owner of the fourth and last private ore jetty, constructed in 1842, and Benjamin Harrison and Montague Ainslie, proprietors of the Newland Company, who owned a blacksmith's shop at Barrow.

The shares were in the main part rapidly taken up, the principal holders being the Duke of Buccleuch, the Earl of Burlington and Benjamin Currey, each with £15,000, the other promoters taking most of the remaining shares. The local ironmasters did not at first offer to take shares, fearing that a railway, controlled almost entirely by the Royalty owners of their mines, might force down their profits by imposing excessive carriage charges. Later, in November 1844, Messrs Harrison and Ainslie agreed to buy some of the remaining shares.

A Bill authorising the construction of the line, with compulsory powers of land purchase, was deposited in the 1843-44 Session of Parliament and without any trouble received the Royal Assent on the 23rd May 1844. The authorised capital was £75,000 with power to borrow £25,000 in loan stock. The line authorised was that previously described and had seven level crossings within the pre-1974 Borough boundary. The time allowed for the completion of the line was seven years, after which time the powers were to lapse.

On the 10th July 1844, the first General Meeting of Shareholders was held at 6 Old Palace Yard, Westminster, the office of Benjamin Currey, the two noblemen sending their representatives. A Board of Directors was appointed consisting of Currey and four other shareholders, Messrs Oddie, Howard, Haworth and Nicholl, Arthur Currey being appointed secretary. The main business was the appointment of an Engineer, and James Walker recommended J R McClean, a junior partner in his practice, also suggesting that J R Wright who had carried out the final survey should be consulted. The final arrangement was left until the Directors Meeting. The shareholders adopted the seal of the Abbey of Furness as the Company Seal and the motto of the Dukes of Devonshire, *Cavendo Tutus* (Secure by Caution), as the Company Motto.

Sir James Ramsden *in later life. Ramsden (1822-1896) joined the Furness Railway as Locomotive Superintendent on 29th January 1846 and retired as Managing Director in 1895. (From North Lonsdale Magazine, Geoff Holme collection)*

At the first Directors Meeting Benjamin Currey was elected Chairman of the Company. The Board then set about the business of land purchase, appointing Thomas Butler of Dalton as valuer and authorising him to proceed at once with negotiations for the purchase of land required for the Barrow-Lindal portion of the line. Later in the month the Directors decided to appoint Messrs McClean and Wright as joint Engineers, their fee being 2.5% of the cost of the line.

Rampside Station, *c.1900. A train for Piel is at the platform. From the opening of the line in 1846 until 1853 this was the end of Furness Railway property. The station building and the adjacent Concle Inn still stand. The station master's house on the left has been replaced by a modern private residence.* (W Anderson collection WH 4.2.2)

Towards the end of July 1844 the Engineers travelled to Furness to carry out the final survey, but in August they reported that the weather had been so unfavourable that they had not been able to complete their work. They did however suggest a new line from Little Mill to Lindal with a lesser maximum gradient of 1 in 100, which involved the construction of Dalton and Lindal tunnels. This could be connected to the Kirkby Branch by a curve at Little Mill. Thus it appears that the Directors were already contemplating through traffic in connection with the proposed Whitehaven and Furness Junction Railway, planned to run from Whitehaven to join up with the Furness just south of Dunnerholme near Ireleth. The W&FJR was authorised in 1845 at a time when the railway mania was beginning.

By September the Engineers had re-surveyed the Barrow portion of the line. It seems probable that the Directors had finally abandoned the idea of horse traction, as this last survey appears to have been with the intention of lessening the gradients and curves. The severe curves of 15 and 20 chains radii at Furness Abbey on the original plan were altered to one curve of 30 chains by building the line through a tunnel to the east of the Abbey, the cost of which was estimated at the incredibly small sum of £300. Had this tunnel not been sanctioned the district's most famous ancient monument would have been endangered.

Another very important alteration to the original plan was the changing of the site of the Barrow terminus. The 1843 plan was for the line to run along the shore to Barrow, then pass through the village to its north end. The line would have followed the course of the present Strand and Fisher Street, terminating where the old Market Hall stood (this is now a car park between Market Street and Cornwallis Street). Instead the terminus was re-located at Rabbit Hill Point. The Barrow Embankment from Salthouse could as a result be built nearer to the coast. There is no reason given for this change but there are several possibilities: the shorter sea embankment would be much cheaper; as the FR board had decided to build its own pier at Rabbit Hill Point rather than use the older jetties of the ironmasters, there was no need to take the line beyond this; and the opposition in the village would no longer be important.

While waiting for the purchase of the land to be completed the Board members were able to sit back and talk about policy. Their main problem was concerned with the order of building the four branches. They also had a few remaining shares to sell, and these were offered to the public as the local ironmasters had shown so little interest. Rail chairs and 65lb. rails were ordered from Messrs Bagnall of West Bromwich. At last Thomas Butler, valuer, reported that the purchase of land between Dalton and Barrow had been completed, and McClean was instructed to invite tenders for the construction of the single line. The line between Dalton and Lindal was deferred because of rapidly increasing costs. At this point Wright resigned from his position as Joint Engineer, being unsatisfied with the arrangement, leaving McClean as Engineer in Charge.

Furness Abbey, north end of Abbey Tunnel, c.1900. The plan of 1843 took the Furness Railway through the Abbey ruins, but in 1845 the Company Engineer J R McClean recommended the tunnel, to reduce the severe curve of the original plan. (E Pouteau, Ken Norman collection)

Crooklands, c.1935. The sidings on the left were the original terminus of the FR in 1846. In the centre is the present main line to Ulverston. On the right is the Stainton Quarry branch built in 1868 to carry limestone from the quarry to Barrow Ironworks. (CRA Pattinson collection 239)

With the coming of the New Year of 1845 the Directors, with the prospect of an early start on the building of the line, renewed their discussion on the order of building. Realising that the Piel line would be quite useless without a functioning Piel Pier, they wrote to John Abel Smith saying they would build their Piel line first if he would give a guarantee to have his Pier ready in time for the opening of the line planned for the early part of 1846. Smith gave this guarantee.

Feeling now that their project was well on the way to becoming a reality the Board proceeded to sanction a series of improvements on the line. The formation was to be for double track between Dalton and Salthouse, £15,000 was to be spent on the new Pier at Barrow and £18,000 on station buildings, carriages and engines. At the Half-Yearly General Meeting on the 26th February 1845, the Board was able to tell the shareholders that Messrs Tredwell's tender of £47,788 19s 6d for the completion of the line by 31st December 1845 had been accepted. Work on the line commenced by building a wooden bridge over the Abbey Beck at Salthouse. The Directors were also able to inform shareholders about the improvements authorised and the increasing traffic expectations, especially in tourist traffic from

Liverpool to the Lakes via Piel. They were also told that the cost of the line would be £108,000 instead of £100,000, that the eastern terminal was to be at Crooklands, east of Dalton, rather than Lindal, and that they proposed to extend to Ulverston as soon as possible.

March 1845 brought the news that the W&FJR were proposing to build a line from Ulverston to Carnforth where a junction was to be made with the Lancaster and Carlisle Railway. The FR Directors resolved to *give every support to a scheme which will give an eastward outlet for traffic and to Mr Robert Stephenson their Engineer* - a strange decision as they would be closed in completely by a foreign company. The decision to make earthworks for double tracks throughout was also made, the Engineer pointing out that the cost of doing this during the building of the line would be only one third that of doing it at a later date.

In May the first trouble arose. Some of the inhabitants of Dalton led by Mr Baldwin presented a petition against the crossing of roads on the level at Little Mill and Goose Green. Although the Company pointed out the many benefits the Railway would confer upon Dalton, the end result was that the original Ruskinville Bridge had to be built near Goose Green at an extra cost of £2,000.

Ruskinville Bridge, 7th May 1954. Just east of Dalton Junction was another of McClean's improvements to avoid a level crossing. Ex-Midland Railway 0-6-0 No. 58299 of Barrow shed (11B) heads for Barrow Yard with a goods train from the Lakeside Branch. The Dalton permanent way gang are putting stone edging to the ballast. (Author MAC 114)

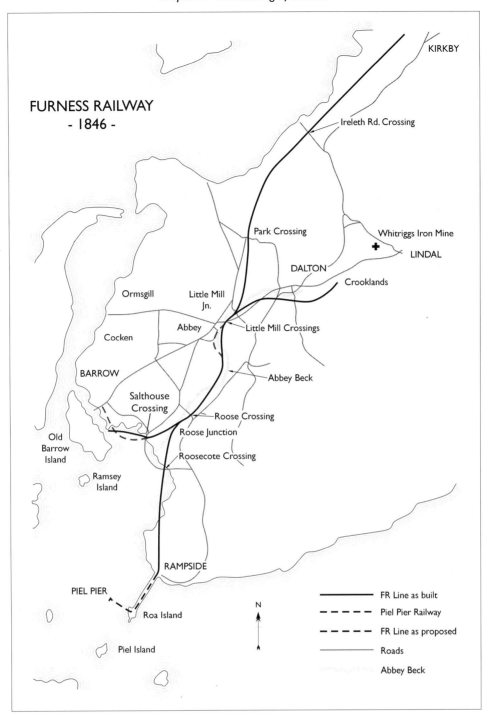

The Earl of Burlington having offered to build an inn adjacent to the Manor House at Furness Abbey, the Board decided that this was an ideal point for an intermediate station, being on the main line and in an attractive position.

Two engines were ordered from Messrs Bury, Curtis and Kennedy of Liverpool at £1,495 each, and 52 wagons were ordered together with three composite first and second class coaches and three all second class. Tolls for iron ore and general goods were settled at 1s 6d (7.5p) and 1s (5p) per ton respectively. The Half-Yearly General Meeting sanctioned the doubling of the earthworks and the application for authority to extend the line from Kirkby to Broughton and from Lindal to Ulverston. The capital was to be increased by £100,000 to pay for this work.

The year 1846 arrived with the line nearly completed, and on the 16th January the Board received a letter from a civil engineer applicant for the post of Superintendent of the Line or Locomotive Superintendent. J R McClean was of the opinion that the post required a person with intimate knowledge of the working of locomotives or of a line of railway, and a civil engineer was not suitable for the job. A second applicant, aged 23, was appointed Locomotive Superintendent on 29th January 1846. His name was James Ramsden, a Bury apprentice who had become a locomotive engineer on the London and Birmingham Railway which used Bury engines. Before the first month of his appointment was out he began to make his presence felt. He proposed an additional embankment from the main line down to the second stage of the pier at Barrow. He also suggested that the other jetties and foreshore at Barrow should be purchased and the Railway Pier gradually extended northwards.

Furness Railway 0-4-0 No 4, c.1898. Just four of these Bury engines operated the F R from 1846 to 1852. (Geoff Holme collection)

Now that the line was nearly ready the Board turned its attention to the buildings required. An engine shed was to be built at Barrow together with a smith's shop. Cottages were to be built at Barrow, Salthouse and Little Mill for the employees of the Company. Although ordered to be constructed as cheaply as possible the cottages built at Rabbit Hill still exist as No 2-20 Salthouse Road. The Pier, which in 1846 had two stages, was built in wood by William Gradwell, a joiner of Roose, and a station was built, also in wood, just east of the Pier on the south side of the present St George's Square.

On the 28th February the Board met John Abel Smith to discuss the details of the operation of the Piel line. Smith said he proposed to run a boat between Fleetwood and Piel twice a day and would build an inn on Roa Island where Piel Pier was being constructed in wood with platforms at three levels. The FR Board said they had decided to build their station on the mainland at Rampside and on the approach of a steamboat a train would proceed to the pier to pick up passengers.

During March a list of tolls was prepared and the facilities offered by the line were advertised, giving the opening date as 1st May. Ore loaders at Barrow, seeing their jobs coming to an end, applied to the Railway Company for employment.

Salthouse Road, Barrow, *c.1960. This terrace of cottages and a similar terrace on the other side of Rawlinson Street were built by the Furness Railway in 1846 to house company employees. Until the establishment of the F R general offices, the topmost cottage was used as an office by Locomotive Superintendent James Ramsden and secretary Arthur Currey. These two terraces still stand.* (F W Cotton)

The line was opened for freight on 3rd June 1846. The Directors Report to the General Meeting of the Company held on 22nd August included the statement: *The line has been partially opened between Dalton and Barrow for goods traffic and the amount of ore carried has equalled the expectations of the Directors considering that the full complement of wagons has not yet been received.* On the 19th August the Board received a letter from the Board of Trade dated 12th August which authorised the FR to commence passenger trains as soon as they thought fit. At the same meeting the Directors learned that John Abel Smith's boat was not ready and that arrangements had been made with John Barraclough Fell of Spark Bridge (who was to become famous for his design of mountain rack railways) to run a steamer between Fleetwood and Piel, for a trial period of two months, the cost of running the services being shared between the FR, Fell and the Preston and Wyre Railway. The Directors ordered that the passenger service should commence immediately. The vessel used was the *Ayrshire Lassie*, which had been chartered by the FR in time for the steamer and passenger trains to commence on 24th August 1846. J B Fell and C M Jopling, agent of the Earl of Burlington, ran omnibus services between Dalton and Windermere and between Kirkby and Coniston in connection with the trains. This faltering start was offset somewhat by the good news that the FR Extension Act had received Royal Assent authorising the building of lines to Ulverston and Broughton.

The Directors met in Furness on the 9th September 1846 to celebrate the opening of the line. There were severe traffic problems on the single line because of the amount of goods traffic, and passenger trains were often subject to delay due to the *Ayrshire Lassie* regularly grounding. After two months the Directors decided to abandon passenger traffic for the year. To make sure that the line would be suitable for a passenger service the next year, the Board authorised the doubling of the line between Millwood Junction and Roose Junction. Although the revenue from passenger traffic at £467 was disappointing, the mineral traffic was satisfactory showing, at the end of the year, a profit amounting to £2,000, and a dividend of 4% p.a. for the half year was declared.

The Directors' main concern in the early months of 1847 was organising the passenger services. Sensing that John Abel Smith was not going to make things easy for them, they decided to meet him to discuss the arrangements at Piel Pier. The meeting was held on 12th May and the FR put forward five alternatives for the working of the pier, varying from the paying of a toll for each train to the lease of the pier for £600 per annum. Smith rejected these suggestions and made two proposals of his own. The first was that he should receive a toll of 1½d (0.625p) per ton and 3d (1.25p) per passenger on all traffic on the FR line, whether loaded at Piel or Barrow! This was of course rejected immediately by the FR. The second proposal was that the amount of the passenger toll should be deducted from the amount due as goods toll but in addition the FR should pay 3d (1.25p) per passenger using Piel Pier. Anxious to come to some agreement the Company quickly accepted this second proposal but omitted to tie Smith down to an opening date.

Furness Abbey Hotel, c. 1869, seen in its heyday. The original Abbey manor house was converted into an hotel in 1847 to the designs of Lancaster architect Edward Paley. Extensions followed during the 1860s. Closed by the LMSR in the 1930s it was demolished c. 1950, apart from the old manor house which remains today as the Abbey Tavern. (*J Payn, Geoff Holme collection*)

FURNESS RAILWAY.

FURTHER OPENING OF THE LINE TO LINDAL,

WITHIN THREE MILES OF THE TOWN OF ULVERSTON.

This line affords the SHORTEST and CHEAPEST route from Maryport, Cockermouth, Workington Whitehaven, Ulverston, and the Lakes.—to Lancaster, Skipton, Leeds, Preston, Liverpool, Manchester, London, &c.

Time Table.—On and after the 1st Nov., 1851,

AND UNTIL FURTHER NOTICE.

Whitehaven to Ulverston, Furness Abbey, Piel, Fleetwood, Lancaster, &c.

UP TRAINS.	WEEK DAYS. 1,2,3 Parl.	1 & 2 class.	1 & 2 class.	1,2,3 class.	1,2,3 class.	SUNDAYS. 1 & 2 class.	1,2,3 class.
	a. m.	a. m.	a. m.	p. m.	p. m.	a. m.	p. m.
Carlisle	..	7 0	..	2 35	..	..	..
Whitehaven, leave	7 0	10 15	..	3 0	7 0	2 30	4 0
St. Bees	7 20	10 28	..	3 16	7 11	2 45	4 14
Sellafield	7 51	10 49	..	5 42	7 37	..	4 37
Seascale	8 0	10 53	..	5 50	7 44	..	4 44
Bootle	8 36	11 21	..	6 25	8 11	..	5 14
Holborn Hill	9 10	11 48	..	7 3	8 43	..	5 43
Broughton, arrive	9 30	12 5	..	7 25	9 0	..	6 0
,, leave	9 40	12 20	..	7 30	9 10	..	6 10
Kirkby	9 50	12 32	..	7 40	9 20	..	6 20
Furness Abbey	10 15	1 0	..	8 0	9 40	..	6 40
Dalton	10 20	1 5	..	8 5	9 50	..	6 50
Lindal	10 30	1 15	..	8 15	10 0	..	7 0
Ulverston, arr.	11 0	1 45	..	8 45	10 30	..	7 30
Ulverston, leave for Piel and the South)	..	12 10					
Lindal	..	12 45	..	..	..	..	..
Dalton	..	12 50	..	..	..	..	..
Furness Abbey	..	1 0	..	..	..	..	..
Barrow	12 20	2 15	..	8 50	10 40	..	7 40
Piel .... arrive	..	1 15	..	..	..	..	..
Fleetwood,	..	..	..	..	..	..	..
,, leave	..			..	..	..	..
Preston	..		..	..	..	..	..
Liverpool	..		..	..	..	..	..
Manchester	..		..	..	..	..	..
Morecambe	..		..	..	..	..	..
Lancaster	..		..	..	..	..	..
Leeds	..		..	..	..	..	..
Birmingham	..		..	..	..	..	..
London	..		..	..	..	..	..

(See Fleetwood Bills)

Fleetwood and Lancaster to Piel, Furness Abbey, Ulverston, Broughton, and Whitehaven.

DOWN TRAINS.	WEEK DAYS. 1,2,3 Parl.	1 & 2 class.	1 & 2 class.	1,2,3 class.	SUNDAYS. 1 & 2 class.	1,2,3 class.
	a. m.	a. m.	a. m.	p. m.	a. m.	p. m.
London	..	8 45	..	..	..	..
		a. m.				
Birmingham	..	12 3	..	..	..	..
Liverpool	..	5 50	..	..	..	..
Manchester	..		..	..	..	..
Preston	..	7 15	..	..	..	..
Leeds	..		..	..	..	..
Lancaster	..		..	..	..	..
Morecambe	..		..	..	..	..
Fleetwood	..	9 0	..	..	..	..
				p. m.	a. m.	p. m.
Piel	..	11 0	..	4 15	..	..
Barrow	..	11 0	..	4 15	7 30	4 20
Furness Abbey	..	11 15	..	4 30	..	..
Dalton	..	11 20	..	..	..	..
Lindal	..	11 30	..	..	..	..
Ulverston, arr.	..	12 0	..	..	..	..
Ulverston for W'haven and the North)	..	10 25	..	3 40	7 35	4 25
Lindal	6 5	11 0	..	4 15	8 10	5 0
Dalton	6 10	11 5	..	4 20	8 15	5 5
Furness Abbey	6 20	11 20	..	4 30	8 25	5 15
Kirkby	6 55	11 45	..	5 10	8 45	5 35
Broughton, arrive	7 5	11 55	..	5 20	8 55	5 45
,, leave	7 15	12 15	..	5 30	9 15	6 15
Holborn Hill	7 34	12 33	..	5 52	9 34	6 34
Bootle	8 4	1 0	..	6 25	9 57	6 57
Seascale	8 36	1 26	..	7 6	10 26	7 26
Sellafield	8 45	1 32	..	7 17	10 33	7 33
St. Bees	9 13	1 53	..	7 55	10 55	7 55
Whitehaven	9 30	2 5	..	8 15	11 15	8 15

BARROW BRANCH.

UP TRAINS.	WEEK DAYS. 1,2,3 class.	1,2,3 class.	1,2,3 class.	1,2,3 class.	1,2,3 class.	SUNDAYS. 1 & 2 class.	1,2,3 class.
	a. m.	a. m.	a. m.	p. m.	p. m.	a. m.	p. m.
Barrow	5 30	8 15	11 0	12 45	5 0	7 30	4 20
Furness Ab.	..	..	11 15	1 0	5 10	7 45	4 35
Dalton	5 45	8 30	..	..	5 15	7 50	4 40
Lindal	5 55	8 50	11 35	1 20	5 30	8 0	4 50
Ulverston	..	..	12 0	1 45	..	10 30	..

BARROW BRANCH.

DOWN TRAINS.	WEEK DAYS. 1,2,3 class.	1,2,3 class.	1,2,3 class.	1,2,3 class.	1,2,3 class.	SUNDAYS. 1,2,3 class.	1 & 2 class.	1,2,3 class.
	a. m.	a. m.	a. m.	p. m.	p. m.	a. m.	p. m.	p. m.
Ulverston	..	9 0	10 25	3 40	..	..	..	..
Lindal	..	9 30	11 50	6 0	8 20	10 10	..	7 20
Dalton	..	9 40	12 0	6 10	8 30	10 15	..	7 30
Furness Ab.	..	9 45	..	..	8 35	10 25	..	7 40
Barrow	..	10 0	12 20	6 30	8 50	10 35	..	7 55
Piel	..	10 30	..	..	..	..	..	..

On Thursdays, Return Tickets will be issued at all Stations for One Fare, to persons attending the Ulverston and Whitehaven Markets.—OMNIBUS FARE:—Lindal to Ulverston, 9d.,—DAY TICKETS, 1s.

General Notices.

On Thursdays, Return Tickets will be issued at all stations for ONE FARE, to persons attending the Ulverston and Whitehaven Markets.

Omnibus Fare:—Lindal to Ulverston, 9d.—DAY TICKETS, 1s.

Return Tickets are issued to 1st and 2nd Class Passengers for ONE FARE AND A HALF on Week-days.

The SUNDAY TRAINS will stop at ROOSE and IRELETH Gates to take up and set down passengers when required.

Passengers from Underhill, Sylecroft, Eskmeals, Ravenglass, Drigg, Braystones and Netherton, will have to re-book at Broughton Station.

Trains leave Whitehaven for Maryport and Carlisle. For particulars see Whitehaven Time Bills.

COACHES to Coniston and Windermere Lakes

Run as follow, in connexion with the Trains (on week days) viz;—from BROUGHTON STATION at 1 p.m., passing through Coniston, Hawkshead, and Ambleside; arriving at the Windermere Railway Station at 5 0 p.m.; and FROM the Windermere Railway Station at 8 a.m., arriving at Broughton at 12 noon.

FARES PER COACH from

Broughton to Coniston .... OUTSIDE 2s.—INSIDE 3s. | Broughton to Ambleside .. OUTSIDE 4s.—INSIDE 5s.
,, Hawkshead .. ,, 3s. ,, 4s. | ,, Birthwaite ,, 5s. ,, 6s.

Barrow, Central Manager's Office,

Nov., 1851.

BY ORDER,

JAMES RAMSDEN.

Furness Railway Time Table, from Soulby's Ulverston Advertiser, 27th November 1851.

(Geoff Holme collection)

On 24th May 1847 passenger trains commenced running again, but as Piel Pier was still not open to traffic the service was to Barrow and the times varied with the tides. However an early opening of the pier was promised and the July *Bradshaw* advertised a regular service to and from Piel with a steamboat service between there and Fleetwood. Earlier in the year the Railway Company had chartered the *PS Helvellyn* of Glasgow for the new regular service of two sailings per day in each direction, as the *Ayrshire Lassie* had proved unsuitable. A train left Kirkby at 6.45 a.m. and joined the 7.00 a.m. from Dalton at Furness Abbey, arriving at Piel in time for the 7.30 a.m. boat to Fleetwood. The *Helvellyn* was to arrive at Fleetwood at 9.00 a.m. and return to Piel at 11.30 a.m., connecting with a train to Dalton and Kirkby. The afternoon sailing was at 4.00 p.m., returning from Fleetwood at 6.00 p.m., with similar connecting arrangements. Indications are that Piel did not open in time even for this service as the September *Bradshaw* shows a reversion to the tidal sailings from Barrow. The *Helvellyn* stopped sailing in September and the Board decided that the Piel Branch would be closed, as the returns did not equal the cost of keeping the line open. It seems possible that a passenger service continued to operate from Barrow during the winter.

During the summer work on the line proceeded smoothly. At Barrow the old Schneider jetty, opposite the Harbour Hotel, was dismantled and replaced by a third stage of the Railway Pier to which a siding had been made. A goods shed was built at Barrow station. By the opening of the passenger service in May the doubling of the line between Millwood Junction and Roose Junction had been nearly completed and Furness Abbey Hotel was almost finished. The double line was opened on 1st June 1847 and the two extensions were proceeding, but whilst the Broughton extension was nearly ready by the end of the year there had been very little progress on the Lindal extension due to the difficult Crooklands rock cutting.

The mineral traffic increased during the summer, but towards the close of the year the iron trade suffered a severe depression, and during 1848 traffic began to fall off. This did not give rise to much concern at first, and at the General Meeting in February 1848 a dividend for the second half of 1847 was declared at 3%. 1848 was notable for the development of the Harbour and of sea traffic, Messrs Fell and Jopling entering into an agreement with the FR by which they chartered the *Helvellyn* for the six months beginning on 1st April. They were to sail twice a day between

Crooklands Cutting, *c.1935, looking west. This cutting, another at Pennington and the Lindal Tunnel delayed the opening of the FR extension to Ulverston until 1854. The FR distant signal is that of Dalton Station box.*
(CRA Pattinson collection PA66)

Lindal Tunnel, *c.1935. The rocky west end of Lindal Tunnel. Completed as a single line bore in May 1851, it was enlarged for double line in 1858 to carry the increased traffic following the opening in 1857 of the Ulverstone & Lancaster Railway.*
(CRA Pattinson collection PA67)

FURNESS ABBEY.

Furness Abbey, c.1860. An early print showing the station and hotel before the rebuilding of the station in 1864 with staggered platforms and a subway. (Geoff Holme collection)

Piel (which was to be open in time for the service) and Fleetwood, the joint undertaking being known as the Liverpool, Fleetwood and Furness Steam Packet Company. A service to Liverpool using the steamer *Zephyr* was started later that year. On 14th August 1848 the FR Amendment Act received Royal Assent. This Act sanctioned an altered route into Ulverston and the raising of a further £100,000 capital. Most importantly the Act authorised the FR to purchase steam vessels to operate between Barrow, Piel Pier and Fleetwood. These powers were obtained in spite of the determined opposition by the Steam Boat Owners Association and a number of shipping companies, the Parliamentary Committee accepting that the Piel-Fleetwood steamer formed an integral part of the FR service. This Act allowed the FR to purchase *Helvellyn* outright.

In the same session the Barrow Harbour Act was passed which enabled the Harbour to be improved, regulated and governed by an appointed Barrow Harbour Commission. The Commissioners were to consist of local landowners, John Abel Smith and the Chairman of the Furness Railway Company. The limits of the Harbour were defined, the northern limit being the North End of Walney and the southern, Westfield Point. The Commissioners were empowered to borrow up to £5,000 from the FR in order to carry out improvements.

In February 1848 the Broughton Extension was completed, but because of building difficulties and the increasing trade depression, work on the Lindal Extension was stopped. Messrs Fell and Jopling's contract was terminated and in compensation they were given quarrying rights in the Crooklands limestone quarry.

Barrow FR General Offices, *April 1955. A side view of the office building and the east end of the engine shed built in 1863 on the site of the original station of 1846. A new large engine shed was constructed further east in 1874, after which this building was used as offices by the Engineers Department, stores and a plumber's workshop. Part of the building still stands.* (Author MAC 34/1)

The year 1848 however saw the first comprehensive passenger service, and analysis of the timetable shows that it could have been worked by two trains starting at Barrow. The exchange station was Furness Abbey, and to connect with the Broughton trains a separate train ran from Dalton to Furness Abbey and back. Omnibus services in connection with the trains ran between Broughton, Coniston and Ambleside and between Dalton and Newby Bridge, operated as before by Fell and Jopling.

In April 1848 the Furness Railway suffered a great and unexpected loss in the sudden death of its Chairman, Benjamin Currey, who had been actively concerned with the line since its promotion. The Earl of Burlington was made a Director and elected Chairman in his place. More trouble was in store however for, with the passing of the months, the depression worsened, traffic fell off still more and the Board was finally frightened into action. Tolls were increased, ore from 1s 6d (7.5p) to 2s (10p) per ton and slate from 2s (10p) to 2s 6d (12.5p) per ton, and a Committee of Investigation consisting of Directors was sent to Furness to inspect the working of the line. The Committee returned from Furness and reported their findings on 21st November. As a result of the Committee recommendations, staff was reduced to an absolute minimum, wages were cut, the pointsman at Roose Junction was discharged and guards were instructed to change the points for their own trains. All gatemen were discharged and gates were to be operated by the wives of Railway employees. As a result of these proposals two cottages were built, one at Salthouse Gate and another at Thwaite Flat Crossing. A curious instruction

was that engines were to be used only *for particular purposes* - perhaps drivers had been in the habit of driving home to Dalton for dinner. The Directors decided to hold a meeting every six weeks at the Furness Abbey Hotel to keep an eye on the line, but they soon seemed to tire of this. The more important changes in policy arising from the crisis were:-

1. *Goods and Mineral traffic shall be primarily considered and provided for and Passenger traffic be only regarded as an auxiliary source of profit.*

2. *When Barrow Pier for steamers is completed no trains shall run to Piel as Passenger Traffic on this line is insufficient to defray expenses.*

Plans were made for the removal of the carriage shed from Rampside to Barrow and Messrs Fell and Jopling's tender of £1,200 for improvements at Barrow Pier was accepted. James Ramsden and Arthur Currey were retained, both at salaries of £200 p.a. to rise to *£250 on the payment of a 3% dividend.*

The next few years were uneventful. Sailings to Liverpool were discontinued in April 1849 and a rival steamboat which had been running between Bardsea and Fleetwood was transferred to Piel in the hope that this might make the Piel Branch pay. In 1849 the steamer agreement with Fell and Jopling was renewed, but on its termination the FR entered into an arrangement with the Lancashire and Yorkshire Railway whereby from 1st November 1849 the two Companies were to share the expense of maintaining the Fleetwood - Piel Service, each providing one steamboat. The FR used the *Helvellyn* and the L&Y the *James Dennistoun*. The *Zephyr* was put up for sale, but the price had to be

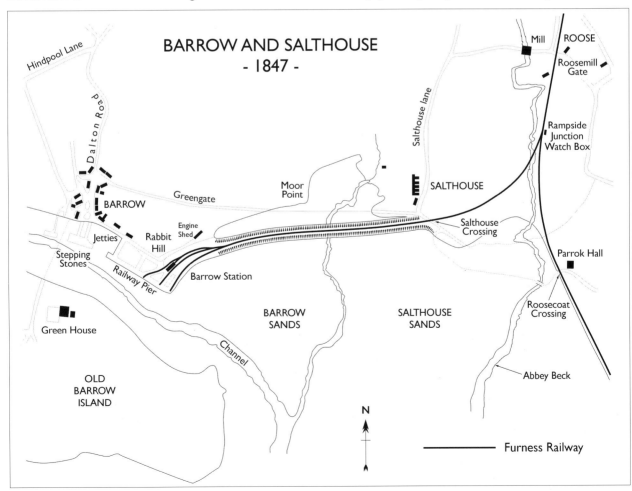

Ulverston Station, *c.1862, showing the original FR terminus of 1854 with the through platforms for the Ulverstone & Lancaster Railway in the foreground. In the centre of the picture is a 3 - position semaphore signal. These platforms were replaced by the present station in 1874, and the imposing original FR terminus was converted to a goods shed. Today it is a car showroom.* (From North Lonsdale Magazine, Geoff Holme collection)

reduced several times before the vessel was eventually sold for £600 in 1850. At Barrow the Rawlinson jetty was removed, the wood being used as engine fire kindling, and the Railway Pier was extended northwards. The Lindal extension was recommenced by a Mr Wheatley in October 1849 but by the middle of 1850 this unfortunate gentleman became bankrupt. Despite being a very sick man he was chased out of Furness by his creditors and, as the story goes, *promptly expired.*

In 1850 the building of a timber wharf enlarged the pier at Barrow still further. At Roose a siding and brickyard were constructed, the owner of the field in which it was built being compensated for the damage: it is interesting to note that the owner of this field was the Chairman of the Furness Railway! In May Arthur Currey resigned from the post of Secretary, and his work was taken over by James Ramsden who was given the title 'Secretary and Manager'. In July the FR suffered its first accident, a collision occurring at Furness Abbey in which a driver was badly injured and a locomotive damaged to the extent of £250. The most important event of the year was the opening, on 1st November 1850, of the Whitehaven and Furness Junction Railway to a junction with the FR near Broughton. In April 1851 the Lindal Extension was completed, Lindal Tunnel being finally finished by Messrs Chappel and Co. Electric Telegraph was installed in this tunnel, and a tender was accepted from Messrs Boulton for the building of the remainder of the line to Ulverston. Opening for passenger traffic to Lindal Road was on 1st June 1851, to Ulverston Road, Lindal on 27th May 1852 and finally to Ulverston on 7th June 1854.

During these years the depression had disappeared and traffic had gradually improved. In 1851 a second joint steamboat service was commenced in conjunction with the (Little) North Western Railway, running between Poulton (later known as Morecambe) and Piel. The dividend, which was stationary at 2% from August 1848 to August 1850,

rose to 3% in August 1852, and passenger traffic was double that of 1848. Mr Smith however once again caused trouble. Hoping to share in the profitable carriage of iron ore he promoted a railway from Lindal to Piel Pier, to be known as the 'Furness and Pile Harbour Railway' and applied to Parliament for a Bill. The Furness Railway immediately organised the strongest opposition. Realising that drastic action must be taken to prevent a recurrence of the troubles of 1846-7, the FR approached Smith with the proposition that the Railway Co. should buy Piel and an independent arbitrator and valuer would set the purchase price. The readiness with which Smith agreed to this proposal suggests that this was possibly his purpose and that the F&PHR was promoted only to precipitate a sale. By this time it was obvious that Piel Pier would never become part of a trunk route and would have to rely on local traffic. Perhaps if Smith had known of the plans of James Ramsden he might not have been as keen to sell out.

J M Rendel, a noted harbour engineer, carried out a survey in December 1852. This was with a view to answering certain questions put to him by the Railway Company concerning the cost of making Piel Pier really efficient and the relative merits of Piel and Barrow as points where shipping could be developed. On 27th December, before Rendel and the arbitrator Swift could present their findings, a violent storm occurred which completely wrecked the property. The rails were broken and swept away from the embankment between Roa Island and the mainland, the goods shed at Roa was blown down and a vessel was driven through the Pier. The FR then refused to accept Captain Rendel's report and negotiations broke down, but after a few months contemplation the FR Board, in April 1853, made Smith an offer of £15,000 for the entire works which he accepted. The FR Act of 1853 authorised the purchase and the necessary increase in Capital. Thus the differences between John Abel Smith and the Furness Railway came to an end.

In the early years, up to 1853, the Furness Railway was mainly concerned with extending its lines to join those projected by its neighbours, the Whitehaven and Furness Junction Railway to the north and the newer Ulverstone and Lancaster Railway to the south. The latter, on the failure of the W&FJR Ulverston to Carnforth scheme Bill on Standing Orders in 1846, had been promoted by John Brogden & Sons, railway contractors of Manchester. They obtained their Act for the construction of a line from Ulverston to Carnforth on the Lancaster and Carlisle Railway in July 1851. While this work was being carried out the hamlet of Barrow was changing. In 1841 it had 17 houses, 4 farms, 2 public houses and a population of 97, but by 1851 the population had risen to 448. The exportation of iron ore had risen from 40,000 tons in 1841 to 200,000 tons in 1851. Henry Schneider discovered enormous quantities of ore at Park, some 3 miles to the north of Barrow. Cottages had been built for the railwaymen at Rabbit Hill in 1846-7 and in September 1849 a school was completed adjoining these cottages. The railway pier, having two stages in 1846, had three in 1847 and then gradually crept northwards along the village shore replacing the older wooden jetties of the ironmasters.

Proposals to bring water to Barrow were first discussed in 1849, and in 1853 a gas works was planned. 1856 saw the beginning of James Ramsden's great scheme for Barrow. He visualised trade expanding at such a rate that by 1870 the population of the town would be 40,000, and prepared a plan for a model town of this capacity. This included 80 foot wide thoroughfares and an area dedicated to industrial development, separate from the residential part of the town, where factories could be sited. It was on this plan that Barrow was later built. Already, other industries were springing up. In 1846, William Gradwell, having built the first wooden railway pier, set up four sheds near the railway station for cutting timber and the manufacture of joinery. In 1855 he moved his works to the Hindpool Industrial Estate where it was known as the Hindpool Sawmills. The site is currently occupied by Hollywood Park. 1847 saw William Ashburner open a ship repair yard at the north end of the village and on 15th September 1852 he launched his first new ship, the *Jane Roper*, for Harrison, Ainslie & Co. In 1852 Henry Schneider was planning the exploitation of the Park ore deposits and he bought screw steamers to carry ore from Barrow Pier to South Wales.

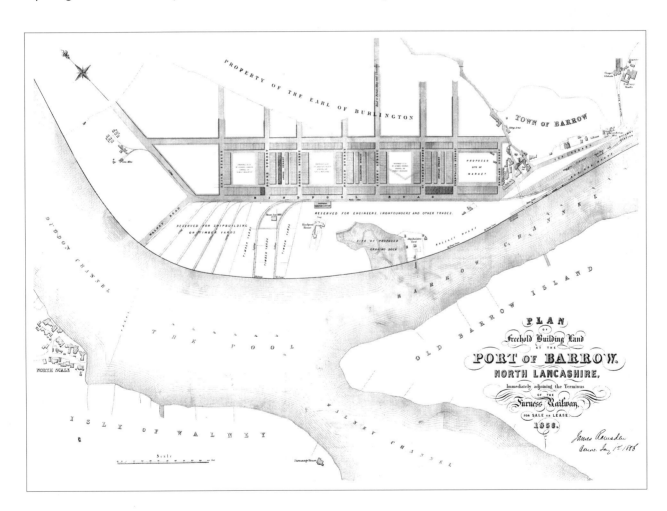

James Ramsden's January 1856 plan. *The purchase of the Hindpool estate north of Barrow village in 1854 encouraged Ramsden to plan for an orderly growth of the town. Hindpool Road, Blake Street and Duke Street enclose a residential area provided with open spaces for 'churches and public buildings'.*
(Based on Cumbria Record Office & Local Studies Library, Barrow. Z537)

Park South, c.1963. An up freight approaches Park South box. The up siding was formerly a goods loop from Park North. Hopper wagons are stored in the down sidings. (J Martin-Hurst, Ken Norman collection)

The development of the port of Barrow began in earnest in 1854. During the previous year the Board had decided that the rail facilities at Barrow must be improved, and they deposited a Bill to authorise a further £50,000 Capital for this purpose. The first improvement was the doubling of the line from Roose Junction to Barrow. A large shore frontage was purchased from the Duke of Buccleuch and 30 more houses were planned. The extensive Hindpool Estate north of Barrow Village was purchased for £7,000 and offices for the Company were built adjoining the station at Rabbit Hill. The Ramsden Plan was adopted and the coastal strip of the Hindpool Estate was set aside for industrial expansion in the town. By July the Schneider screw steamers had commenced running to South Wales and by September the doubling of the line was complete. Two steam tugs were purchased for the Harbour. The first iron foundry in Barrow was opened on Salthouse Marsh, situated near the present Foundry Street, and later became known as Briggs Foundry.

General Offices, St Georges Square, c.1860. Edward Paley's plans for the first phase of the building.
(Cumbria Record Office & Local Studies Library, Barrow)

Barrow Pier, *c.1864. A view looking south from the embankment enclosing the Devonshire Dock and providing the road to Old Barrow Island. Barrow Pier was enclosed by the Salthouse embankment in 1870 to form the Buccleuch Dock. The High Level bridge was built over this enbankment and opened in May 1882.* *(From North Lonsdale Magazine, Geoff Holme collection)*

On other parts of the line progress was also being made. The repairs to the Piel Branch were completed early in the year, and sidings were built on the main line at Park, just north of Thwaite Flat, to serve the new mines of Messrs Schneider and Davis. On the 7th June 1854, after years of struggle with the difficult cuttings near Swarthmoor, the Ulverston Extension was opened to passenger traffic, having been open to freight since 4th April. Electric Telegraph was installed the same year on the entire system. The dividend for the half year was declared at 6% p.a.

Following on the enterprise of 1854, two Acts were passed in 1855. The first, the Furness Railway Act 1855, repealed previous Acts, united the Railway, Pier and Steamboats and increased the Capital to £340,000. The second Act was obtained by the Barrow Harbour Commissioners and authorised them to borrow a further £30,000 from the FR Company, which was to be used to carry out improvements at the Harbour. £9,000 was lent in this year and the dredging of Barrow Channel commenced. It had already become obvious that, as soon as through running commenced, the single line to Ulverston would be inadequate, and in 1855 doubling of this part of the line, which included the widening of Lindal Tunnel, was started. Although there had been a slight falling off in traffic during the year due to a depression resulting from the Crimean war, the dividend was maintained at 6%.

Park North signalbox, crossing house *and an inclined plane serving the North Pit of Park iron mine. This box, replacing an older one, was built in 1883 to the design of Paley & Austin. A number of similar boxes date from this period. The signal for the up loop carries a ring denoting a goods line. These rings were removed in 1896.* *(Dock Museum, Barrow)*

Dalton Junction, April 1954. Black 5 4-6-0 45451 of Carlisle Upperby shed (12A) runs onto the Dalton Loop Line with a Carnforth - Carlisle freight. The first part of the 'Loop' was the Millwood Curve of 1858 planned to avoid the reversal of through trains at Furness Abbey. *(Author MAC 122)*

The next three years saw increasing prosperity. Traffic expanded so much during 1856 that at the year-end, in addition to paying a 6% dividend, £2,000 was set aside out of profits to rebuild part of Barrow Pier in masonry. On 10th August 1857 the Ulverstone and Lancaster Railway was opened for goods traffic, thus connecting the Furness system with the railways of Lancashire and Yorkshire. Anticipating an increase in through traffic, plans were made for doubling the line from Millwood Junction to Park and for the construction of a curve at Millwood to give direct access to the north from Ulverston. This work was commenced towards the end of 1857, and on 1st July 1858 the new double line curve, the Millwood Curve,

was opened between Dalton Junction at Goose Green and Park (later Goldmire) Junction on the Broughton Branch. A similar curve was built at Foxfield.

The passenger service had gradually increased over the years, and in 1858 there were eight down and nine up trains daily. The *Helvellyn* had been sailing three times a week during winter as well as twice a day during the summer, but after the opening of the Ulverstone and Lancaster Railway the ship was laid up during the winter because of the alternative route available. Passengers travelling through to Whitehaven did not use the Millwood Curve, changing instead at Furness Abbey into trains from Barrow to Broughton.

FR 2-2-2 tank No. 21. *The FR aquired three pairs of these sturdy little passenger engines, 5 & 6 in 1852, 11 & 12 in 1857 and 21 & 22 in 1864. After the arrival of the 2-4-0s in 1870, they were relegated to branch line work. Prior to 1852 all traffic was handled by the four Bury 0-4-0s.* *(George Taylor collection)*

The year 1859 saw the establishment of an industry that was to turn the little port of Barrow into a rapidly expanding industrial centre. Henry Schneider and his new partner Robert Hannay of the Park iron mines had approached the Furness Railway Company in 1857 with a view to purchasing land near Barrow on which to erect blast furnaces. The Company suggested James Ramsden's proposed industrial estate at Hindpool, which Schneider and Hannay agreed was a convenient site for an iron-works, and in the latter part of 1858 they decided to buy the northern part of the estate. Agreement was reached with the Furness Railway Co. early in 1859, and on 19th October the first two blast furnaces were blown in. The same year saw the establishment of the Furness Brick and Tile Co.'s works near Ormsgill.

The Railway itself continued to expand and on 18th June 1859 the Coniston Railway from Broughton to Coniston was opened, being worked by the FR. Also, during 1859 the hotel at Furness Abbey station was enlarged.

Traffic increased steadily during the next few years and the Hindpool ironworks expanded. By February 1860 three furnaces were working, and by the end of 1861 six had been built. When the ironworks were opened the nearest rail-point was the north end of Barrow sidings, and the Railway Company soon realised that they must gain access to the new works. A track relaying programme of 1860 left the Company with several miles of used iron rails, so a tramway was built along the shore from the north end of the railway pier to the works, using these old rails. To accommodate the increasing ore traffic to the works, the sidings at Park, Lindal and Barrow were enlarged.

In 1861 a Bill was deposited which, besides enabling the FR to increase its capital by a further £160,000, authorised the construction of a branch which was to pass through Hindpool and continue on to Hawcoat Quarry. The part of the branch between Barrow and the ironworks had already been built, but the purpose of the extension to Hawcoat Quarry, leased by the FR from the Duke of Buccleuch, was to obtain red sandstone for building, which at that time had to be brought in from a distance of over fifty miles. Many of the railway buildings dating from this period are in sandstone, and it is very likely that Ramsden already had in mind the dock schemes, which would require large amounts of stone, although these were not announced until the following year. The Bill was also to seek authority for the purchase of the Ulverston Canal for £22,000, the expenditure of £25,000 on new steam vessels and to provide additional steamer services. In spite of opposition from the Liverpool and Irish shipping companies, the Act received Royal Assent on 30th June 1862. Although powers to operate shipping services were renewed, these were limited to Barrow and Fleetwood, a proposed service to Belfast being rejected.

Hindpool, April 1955. Ex-Midland Railway 0-6-0 58287 of Barrow shed (11B) runs light on the short section of main line between Hindpool North and Hindpool South signal boxes. On the left are the furnaces of Barrow Ironworks and on the right the edge of the steelworks. (Author MAC 72)

Even as this Act was passing through Parliament, Ramsden was embarking on the scheme that was to make him famous and which was also the other big factor in the development of Barrow. Barrow Harbour had been controlled nominally by the Barrow Harbour Commissioners since the Act of 1848, but non-railway members had ceased to attend the meetings after the first few years. This, and the fact that the finances of the Commissioners had always been shaky (having had to rely on the railway company for loans in order to carry out improvements), were used by Ramsden as reasons in favour of the first step in his scheme, the vesting of the Barrow Harbour in the Furness Railway Company. The second step was to overcome the main disadvantage of Barrow Harbour, the fact that it was tidal. This was to be accomplished by the building of a dock between Barrow Island and the mainland, created by closing the south end of Barrow Channel with an embankment, and having an entrance lock at the north end. The embankment was to run from Salthouse to the southern tip of Barrow Island, thus enclosing, as well as the Channel, a stretch of sand south of the old railway embankment that could be used as a timber float. The final part of the scheme was an agreement with the Midland Railway, in October 1862, that a Joint Line should be built from Wennington, on the Midland's Skipton-Morecambe line, to Carnforth. Using this line, all Midland Railway traffic to Belfast and the Isle of Man would run to Barrow instead of to Morecambe. There was an understanding, never ratified as a formal agreement, that the FR would not extend east of the Lancaster and Carlisle line and that the Midland would not extend west of it. There was to be an exchange of running powers, the Furness to run to Leeds and Bradford and the Midland to Piel and Barrow. McClean and his assistant F C Stileman prepared plans for the new dock and the Joint Line. Bills seeking authority for these schemes were deposited in 1862.

Three main petitioners opposed the Dock Bill. The Mersey Docks and Harbour Board and the Port of Lancaster Trustees and Commissioners, seeing that a new dock on the North West Coast would take some of their traffic, registered strong disapproval, pointing out the adequacy of the existing ports. The third source of opposition was the Earl of Lonsdale. His interest lay in the navigation of the Duddon Channel, and he was pacified by the insertion of the phrase *providing no injury to the Duddon Channel* into the Bill. The Duke of Devonshire (formerly Earl of Burlington), as Chairman of the Furness Railway Company, satisfied the Parliamentary Committee that the dock was necessary to accommodate the shipping engaged in local trade. He made the point that the population of Barrow and district had risen from 200 in 1846 to 7,000 and that the present harbour was tidal. The fact that the Harbour Commissioners could not make enough profit from dues and had to borrow large sums from the Railway in order to carry out any improvements was used as evidence. McClean appeared in person to give an account of the dock and estimated the cost at £100,000.

The efforts of the Furness Board were not in vain, and on 22nd June 1863 the Furness Railway and Barrow Harbour Act duly received Royal Assent. The Act transferred the rights of the Commissioners to the Railway Company and sanctioned the building of a dock and other works at Barrow, giving the FR jurisdiction over the Piel Channel as far as Helpsford Scar to the south and Scarth Channel to the north. The increase in capital was £137,000.

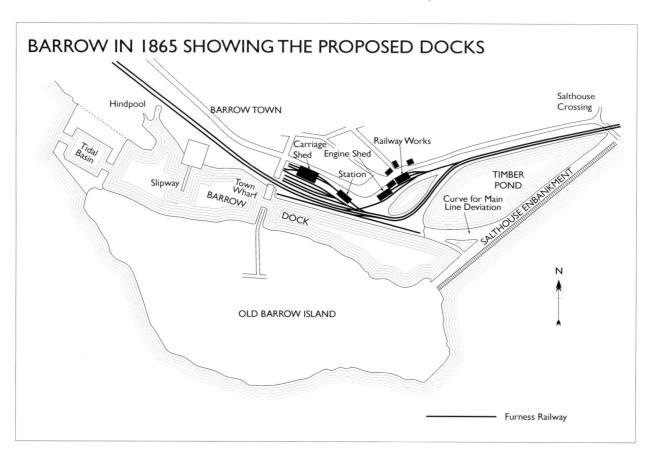

BARROW IN 1865 SHOWING THE PROPOSED DOCKS

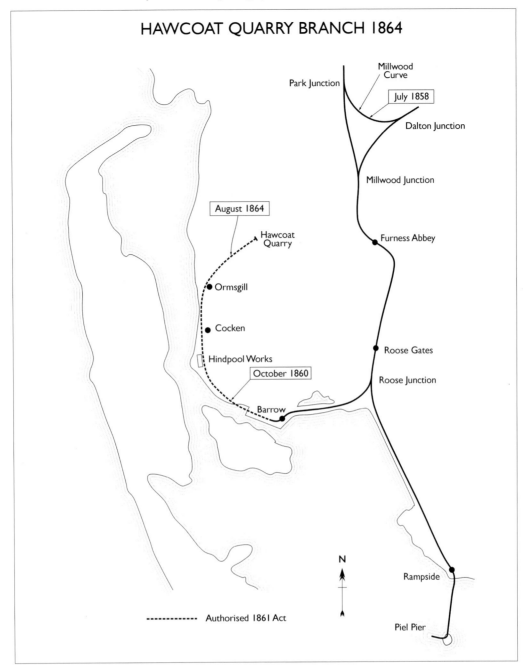

HAWCOAT QUARRY BRANCH 1864

Meanwhile these years saw Barrow expanding at an ever-increasing rate. The remaining wooden part of the pier was rebuilt in stone, £3,000 worth of new sidings were put down, a goods shed was built at the north end of the pier and the school at Rabbit Hill was enlarged at Railway Company expense. The development of the ironworks caused fresh interest in a water supply scheme for Barrow, which had been first discussed in 1849 and then shelved. Water was necessary for the works, and the FR Board proposed that some of the money obtained from the sale of the ironworks site should be used to build a reservoir and water main. A reservoir was built in the hills behind Ireleth and by February of 1863 the water main had been laid to Furness Abbey: it reached Barrow in March.

The population was increasing so rapidly that it was decided that the existing station at Rabbit Hill was no longer large enough, and, on 28th February 1862, plans drawn by Edward Paley, the Lancaster architect, for a new station in St George's Square were shown to the Directors. These were approved and tenders were invited. The work was let in parts to various local firms, the total being £2,233, and a carriage shed was built nearby for £600. The new station was opened on 29th April 1863. The original wooden station was demolished and the site used for a new engine shed built of sandstone. This later station building still stands (with some alterations) and a long wall was built to separate the Railway from the Strand. At the northern end of the wall four houses were built, in two pairs, for the Harbour Master, Pier Master, Ballast Master and Goods Agent. Each pair was built with the two houses facing each other across a courtyard, which was reached by high arches in the wall. The wall and the four houses, together with the former stables later converted to a motor repair workshop, were still to be seen until July 2002 forming the west side of the Strand, when they were demolished to make way for a supermarket. In 1872, after the station had become inadequate to deal with increasing traffic, the carriage shed was converted to an arrival station, a new carriage shed being built.

29

Barrow Strand, *April 1955. In 1862-3 the Furness Railway enclosed its land on Barrow foreshore by a long wall from the new station of 1863 to the factories in Hindpool Road. Inside this were built two pairs of houses with access to the Strand by arches. They were occupied by railway officers. The northernmost pair looks onto the Ship Hotel closed in 1964.* (Author MAC 38/2)

Barrow Station of 1863, *7th July 1968. Designed by architect Edward Paley the Strand station replaced the original wooden building of 1846. On the opening of Ramsden Dock station in 1881 the Strand station was designated Barrow Town in the public timetables. It was closed on 1st June 1882 on the opening of Barrow Central station on Abbey Road. It became the Cambridge Hall available for functions but in recent years has been a railway staff club. Barrow Train Control office occupied the left hand end of the building from 1918.* (Author MAA 726)

On the opening of Barrow Central station in 1882 this converted building became in turn the Drill Hall, the Palais dance hall and a Tenpin Bowling alley. Following a fire in the 1970s the roof was replaced and what remained of the building converted to the Bowater Social Club. After this closed, the building was sold to the British Working Men's Club and re-opened in August 1996. This has also been demolished to make way for the new supermarket development. The 1863 station, now a listed building, still standing in St. George's Square, after 1882 housed the Cambridge Hall, a Furness Railway Staff Institute and now houses the Railway Club.

Before the building of the Hawcoat Branch and the new station, access to the Pier and Goods Yard had been by means of a curve on the seaward side of the old station. The scar, which had been cut at Rabbit Hill for the original line, was used for an extension of the Railway General Offices, and the building bore on its date-stone, 1864. This well known Barrow landmark was demolished in stages from 1976 to 1978.

As owners of the Hindpool Estate the Furness Railway held the land on which the main part of the new town was being built and, for the convenience of local traders, the Company decided, in 1862, to build a Market Hall and Public Rooms. These were started in 1863, and a Police building was added to house the Police Force which the rapidly expanding town found very necessary. These buildings were familiar to older Barrovians as the Market Hall, Public Hall and Police Station. The Police Station was replaced by the present building in the late 1950s and the Market Hall by the new structure on Duke Street, opposite the Town Hall, which was opened by HM the Queen on 10th June 1971. The old building was quickly pulled down and is now the site of a car park and Town Square bordered by the Town Hall and by Market, Lawson and Cornwallis Streets. The Public Hall, originally the town's first Town Hall, was demolished in 2000 to make this new public area possible. The statue of Lord Frederick Cavendish, for many years a Furness Railway Director until his assassination in Dublin in May 1882, was relocated to this square.

During 1863 and 1864 the Hawcoat Quarry branch was built, the southern portion following the course of the 1860 tramway, and sidings were put in at the Ironworks. Passing just east of the works and turning north to pass the new Furness Brick and Tile Co.'s works, the line turned north-east and climbed at 1 in 45 on an embankment up to the quarry. Just over 2 miles 2 furlongs long, the line, double as far as the Ironworks sidings and single beyond, was in use by the summer of 1864. In the 1870s the original embankment was abandoned, and a higher one built about 20 yards to the south to give more clearance over Schneider Road and to enable a high part of the quarry to be reached. This road crossing was to the north of the present St Francis' Church.

The prosperity of the company continued to increase. The dividend had remained at 8% from 1860 to 1863 but in 1864 10% was paid on the ordinary shares for the first time. The Company, as well as being successful commercially, had contrived to extend its territory still further. The Ulverstone and Lancaster Railway Company, always in financial difficulties, had to borrow to the extent of £30,000 from the Duke of Buccleuch and the then Earl of Burlington in order to complete their line. The lease of the line to the FR was talked of during 1861, and at a meeting at Chatsworth on 9th November agreement was reached on the takeover of the line by the Furness, powers for which were included in the 1862 Act. The line was transferred to the FR on 21st January 1862, and the latter Company proceeded to double the line throughout, this work being completed through to Carnforth in August 1863. On the 7th July 1862 the Coniston Railway was similarly absorbed.

Another important line which was of great value to the Furness area was opened in 1861. This was the South Durham and Lancashire Union Railway, which connected the Durham coal field with the iron mines and blast furnaces of the west coast. It was coke from Durham which was an important factor in the rapid expansion of the Barrow Ironworks and the creation of the steelworks, opened in 1865. The SD&LUR running through Barnard Castle and over Stainmore, joined the Lancaster and Carlisle line at Tebay.

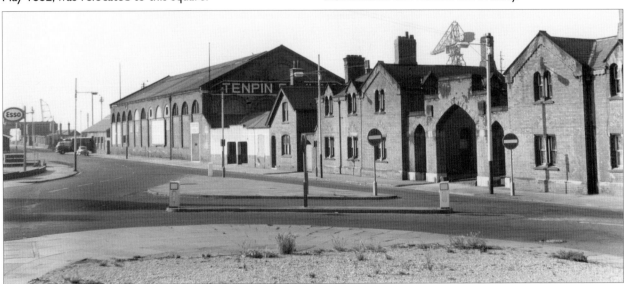

Barrow Strand, 7th July 1968, showing the southernmost pair of officers' houses and the carriage shed of 1863. To increase the capacity of the FR Barrow Station, this building was converted into an arrival station in 1872. Since the opening of Barrow Central station in 1882 this building has been a rollerskating rink, the Palais ballroom and a tenpin bowling alley. About 1980 it was partly demolished for the building of the Bowater Scott social club and the site is now part of Morrisons Supermarket. Only the arch on the right of the picture now remains. (Author, MAA 727)

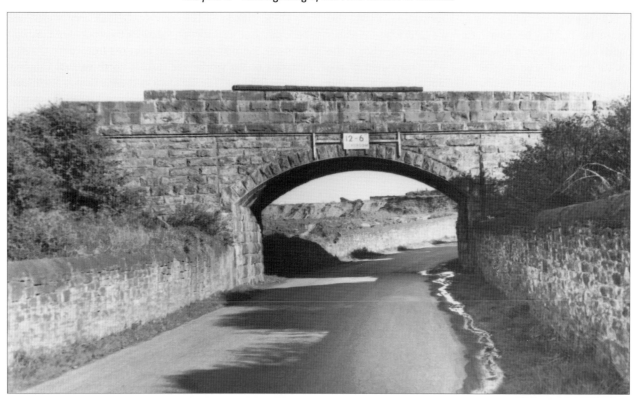

Hawcoat Quarry branch bridge, *c.1963. This bridge over the north end of Walney Road was built in 1864 to carry the original Hawcoat Quarry branch. When the branch was severed by the Barrow Loop Line the new connection from Cocken Junction used the bridge. It remained standing for many years after the Hawcoat Branch closed c.1930, but was swept away during the construction of the new A590 Park Road in the early 1980s.* (Author MAA 63)

Hawcoat Quarry, *c.1909. George Romney's early home had recently been refurbished by the Furness Railway.* (Authors collection)

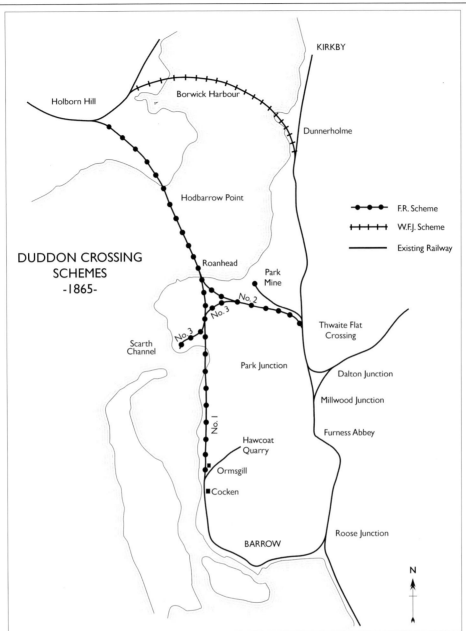

During the early 1860s the Furness Railway had managed to annex two of its neighbours easily, but the last remaining independent line, the Whitehaven and Furness Junction Railway, was only taken over after considerable difficulty.

The cause of the dispute between the two companies was the Duddon Crossing Scheme which the W&FJR was planning. The FR Directors decided, on 20th October 1864, to apply for a Bill for a Duddon Viaduct, but in the same month the W&FJR deposited a similar Bill. Edward Wadham, mineral agent of the Duke of Buccleuch and acting agent of Lord Lonsdale, writes in his diary that he talked with James Ramsden about the W&FJR Scheme on 26th September, but he does not say whether or not Ramsden already had plans for a FR crossing. It is possible that Ramsden heard of the W&FJR plan and immediately had a rival FR plan drawn up. On depositing their Bill the W&FJR asked the FR to give them financial support for their scheme. By way of persuasion, the W&FJR added that, if the FR did not support their scheme, they would disregard the Furness altogether

and build their line across to Lindal, thus completely avoiding Barrow with its new docks under construction. As the W&FJR plan avoided Barrow anyway, the FR Board turned down the request for support. The W&FJR Scheme, from Millom to Dunnerholme, was to join the FR main line at Ireleth. Traffic from this line would have to travel all the way round via Millwood Junction, Furness Abbey and Salthouse to reach Barrow. The FR Bill planned to bring the traffic nearer to Barrow on a viaduct from Hodbarrow to Roanhead, the line then continuing directly south to Ormsgill to join the Hawcoat Branch (No. 1 on map). Through traffic to the east was to be carried on a second line from Roanhead to Thwaite Flat, which would have joined the main line just south of Park South level crossing (No. 2). A spur between these two lines (No. 3) would have given direct access to the Ironworks from Park Mines, a valuable asset to the Company, as the congestion caused at Barrow Station by the ore traffic from Park having to run round via Salthouse to the Ironworks was becoming acute.

Henry Schneider, proprietor of Park Mines and Barrow Ironworks, appeared before the House of Commons Committee which was investigating the two schemes, and strongly supported the Furness proposal. The W&FJR scheme had a great advantage over the Furness one in that the former, being farther north, did not block the channel to the little port of Borwick Rails where ore from Hodbarrow Mine was loaded. The existence of this port meant that the Furness had to include a 36ft opening span in their 2618 yards long viaduct. The opposition now said that traffic on the FR viaduct would be held up for considerable periods at high tide in order to allow the shipping on the Duddon to pass through. Schneider replied that Hodbarrow ore could be carried by rail to Barrow by the FR line and thus shipping would no longer need to go to Borwick which, in his opinion, was so dangerous a port that he refused to allow his own vessels to go there. The remainder of the Committee stage was taken up by a comparison of the cost of sending ore from Borwick to Barrow by rail for shipment and of shipping it direct from Borwick. The result of this comparison was that the Furness lost the fight and the W&FJR Scheme was passed. The Furness was left with powers to build a loop from Park to the Hawcoat Branch, with a short branch to the shore at Scarth Point, their Bill receiving the Royal Assent on 29th June 1865. The Furness realised that there was only one course to take, and, even before the W&FJR Bill had received Royal Assent, Devonshire had met Lonsdale and the lease of the W&FJR to the FR at 8% had been arranged. The line became part of the FR on 1st July 1866.

It seems, however, that there might have been more than two parties involved. Rumour had it that the Midland Railway were planning a West Coast approach to Scotland via the FR, the W&FJR and the Maryport and Carlisle Railway. At this time, before the building of the Settle to Carlisle line, they were having great difficulty with their Scottish traffic. It had to be run over the Lancaster and Carlisle line, and the London and North Western Railway were killing the traffic by poor connections. It was suggested that the reason the MR agreed to promote the Wennington Joint Line with the Furness, and to divert all their Irish and Isle of Man traffic to Barrow, was that it wanted the Furness line for its Scottish route.

The rumour is discredited by the fact that, as early as the second meeting of the Furness and Midland Joint Committee on 18th February 1864, the Midland Directors had indicated that they wished to withdraw their support for the Barrow Dock Scheme. On learning that the Furness intended to carry on, even without Midland support, they agreed to go through with the plan. This deterioration in Furness and Midland relations occurred a long time before either of the Crossing Schemes had been planned. Also, and more significantly, the Midland and the London and North Western Railways were looking at joint use of the Lancaster and Carlisle line between Low Gill and Carlisle. The breakdown of these negotiations, which led to the Settle and Carlisle line proposal, came after the 1865 Agreements between the LNWR, the FR and the various West Cumberland railway companies. The purpose of the Whitehaven and Furness Junction Railway's Duddon Crossing scheme seems now to have been a reduction in mileage between West Cumberland and the iron trade markets in the Midlands and Wales rather than part of a secret agenda for a Midland Railway West Cumberland route to Scotland.

General Offices, *1955. This building, built in stages, was completed in the 1860s. On the right is the engine shed constructed on the site of the passenger platform of 1846. The west end of the engine shed was altered to make a porter's lodge. Most of this building still stands, while the general offices have been demolished.*
(Author MAC 33)

On 20th October 1863, the Dock Scheme was launched with the acceptance of Messrs Brassey and Field's second and lower tender of £132,970 14s 0d and the purchase of Barrow Island from the Michaelson family. By August of the following year, work on the Salthouse Embankment had started (this would enclose the Buccleuch Dock), and work was beginning on the entrance lock and tidal basin of the Devonshire Dock at Hindpool. Ramsden planned to divert the main line onto the new embankment at Salthouse, so this was constructed at rail level and 28ft wide to carry double track. Hydraulic apparatus for the Dock Gates was supplied by Sir William Armstrong and Co. in August 1866, and on 1st August 1867 the tide was admitted to the completed Devonshire Dock.

The years 1864-67 saw continuing prosperity and development: a 10% dividend was maintained and the capital was considerably increased. Furness Abbey Station reached its final form by the removal of the old station master's house and the building of a subway and island platform in 1864. The expansion of the Furness Abbey Hotel was completed by 1866. The engine shed at Barrow was enlarged and a Wagon Repair Shop built on reclaimed land inside the main line. The Locomotive Works on Salthouse Road was extended and, in order to accommodate the staff of the W&FJR, the Offices at the south side of St George's Square were enlarged again in 1866. A house at Salthouse, now the

site of the United Club and Institute near the corner of Friars Lane and Roose Road, was bought at a cost of £1,800 for Henry Cook, Secretary of the W&FJR, who became Secretary and Traffic Manager of the Furness after the take-over in 1866. Warehouses were built on the dockside costing £3,000. Most of these buildings have now been pulled down: Furness Abbey Hotel, apart from the original portion which is now the Abbey Tavern, was demolished in 1953, and the station followed soon after. The Wagon repair shop was pulled down in 1978 shortly after the General Offices. Parts of the locomotive works, including the Erecting Shop have survived and are now known as Davey's Yard.

The year 1866 saw the passing of another Act of Parliament, its main contents being the W&FJR absorption and the building of the Newby Bridge and Stainton branches. As the Company was finding the large number of level crossings on the line an increasing embarrassment, there was a section in the Act authorising the building of bridges and the stopping up of some of the crossings. The largest scheme was the Salthouse and Roosecote Road Diversions. At this time road traffic for Rampside went along Salthouse Road, which had been built along the north side of the original railway embankment from Rabbit Hill to Salthouse. It crossed the line onto the sand at Salthouse Crossing, which was situated just east of the present Sandgate Hotel, and then followed the coast. Traffic for Roosecote crossed

Barrow Works, c.1920. This aerial view shows on the left the Strand station, the General Offices, the locomotive works and the chimney in Salthouse Road. In the centre is the carriage & wagon works with its tower. On the far right is the locomotive shed of 1874.   *(George Taylor collection)*

Roose station, c.1935. Looking west towards the Roose Road bridge built c.1873 by the FR. (CRA Pattinson collection PA88)

the Abbey Beck on a bridge and the Piel Branch over Roosecote Crossing at Parrock Hall. At Roose station there were originally two crossings, but by 1866 the Roose Mill Crossing had been closed, leaving only that at Flass Lane, the crossing house of which survived until the last war, when it was bombed and had to be pulled down. The plan was to replace these crossings by one bridge south of the station (the present Roose Bridge), and to build a road from Salthouse to Roosecote via this bridge. Associated with this scheme was a plan to divert the Abbey Beck into the new timber pond, which would be enclosed with the

completion of the Salthouse Embankment. A cut was authorised by the Act of 1867 to run along the north side of the main line from Roose and then to pass under the road at Salthouse Crossing to enter the proposed pond.

The smaller scheme was the elimination of the two crossings at Millwood Junction. As things were, the Barrow-Dalton Road crossed the line about 100 yards south-west of the junction, and Millwood Lane left this road on the Dalton side of the crossing, therefore having to re-cross the line just at the junction. A new road, 80ft wide to match the other Barrow main roads, was to be built crossing the

Salthouse, c.1920. Aerial view of the Paper Mills opened in 1880, with the Barrow gasworks opened in 1919 behind. The Stank Branch climbs into a cutting, and curving away on the left is the main line between Salthouse Junction and Roose.   (George Taylor collection)

line just north east of the old main road on a wide bridge, the present Millwood Bridge. The new Millwood Lane was to leave the main road on the Barrow side of the new bridge.

These works proceeded very slowly, taking until 1874 to complete, the actual bridge not being commenced until 1872. The Millwood diversion was completed on the lines planned, and the original main road is still used on the Dalton side of the old crossing. It forms the Dalton end of the 'Low Road' between Furness Abbey Station and Little Mill Cottages. The site of the Barrow side of the old road may still be seen as a narrow cutting leading up from the railway on the south west side of the present bridge. The original Millwood Lane ran between the old crossing house and a bungalow built on the site of the goods shed and the signal box with its interesting octagonal base. The crossing house, which is still occupied, retains its garden wall and gate onto the old road. The Salthouse scheme took longer, and by the time the Roose Road was built, a new Act was needed as, in the meantime, the layout of the railway had altered considerably (see plan on page 54).

Although the passenger traffic had not become much heavier, the first half of the decade saw striking changes in the timetable. The 1860 timetable was for trains from Barrow and Piel to Ulverston and Coniston. The trains ran from Barrow to Furness Abbey and then on to either Coniston or Ulverston. Passengers between Ulverston and Broughton or Coniston changed at Furness Abbey, as did passengers for Piel and Fleetwood.

Between 1860 and 1864 the timetable changed. Now Carnforth to Whitehaven became the main line, with Furness Abbey to Barrow labelled the 'Barrow Branch' and Furness Abbey to Piel, the 'Piel Branch'. Furness Abbey Station, however, remained the exchange station and trains for Whitehaven reversed here. In connection with these through trains a train ran out from Barrow to Furness Abbey and back. The service in connection with the Fleetwood boats ran from Barrow to Piel and back, reversing at Furness Abbey in the passenger-carrying direction and, presumably, at Roose when returning empty. The *Helvellyn* sailed once per day in each direction, arriving from Fleetwood at 12 noon and returning at either 2.20 p.m. or 4.15 p.m. The train time between Barrow and Piel via Furness Abbey was 40 minutes. When a halt was built at Roose Crossing in the 1850s, Roose Junction had been moved eastwards to Roose Crossing Gates and the single track Piel Branch ran parallel to the main line through the site of the present Roose Station before diverging to the south.

By 1865 a second steamer, the *Myrtle*, was running six days a month between Piel and the Midland Pier at Morecambe.

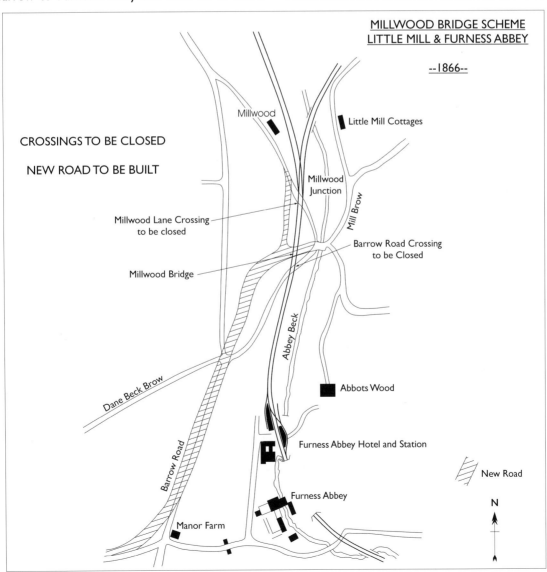

MILLWOOD BRIDGE SCHEME
LITTLE MILL & FURNESS ABBEY

--1866--

CROSSINGS TO BE CLOSED

NEW ROAD TO BE BUILT

Millwood

Little Mill Cottages

Millwood Junction

Mill Brow

Millwood Lane Crossing to be closed

Barrow Road Crossing to be Closed

Millwood Bridge

Abbey Beck

Dane Beck Brow

Abbots Wood

Barrow Road

Furness Abbey Hotel and Station

New Road

Furness Abbey

N

Manor Farm

Crooklands, *c.1935.*
Looking west to Dalton station with the Stainton Quarry branch, on the left, opened in 1868. This line remained in operation until 12th October 1966 (CRA Pattinson collection PA75)

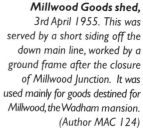

Millwood Goods shed,
3rd April 1955. This was served by a short siding off the down main line, worked by a ground frame after the closure of Millwood Junction. It was used mainly for goods destined for Millwood, the Wadham mansion. (Author MAC 124)

Furness Abbey station, *c.1910. On the right is the low-level booking office next to the subway. On the left is the down island platform where originally exchange between Barrow and Whitehaven trains took place.* (Ken Norman collection KNO 968)

The year 1867 was arguably the most spectacular Barrow has ever known. J Richardson, author of 'Furness Past & Present', writing in 1876, looked back upon 1867 as the *red letter year in the history of Barrow*. The 'Man of the Year' was undoubtedly James Ramsden. Work on his Dock Scheme had, between 1864 and 1867, nearly doubled the population of the town. Standing at over 3,000 before the Scheme in 1861, by 1864 it was 6,000 and by 1867 11,000, the immigrants being either 'navvies' employed by Messrs Brassey and Field or steelworkers for the expanding iron and steel industry. In addition to the Dock Scheme, Ramsden had, on behalf of the Railway Company, its Directors and the Ironworks Proprietors, opened the Barrow Steel Company's Bessemer Plant adjacent to the Ironworks at Hindpool. The union of these two companies, in 1866, created the Barrow Haematite Steel Company, who paid a massive 30% dividend the following year. Ramsden had, moreover, been elected to the Furness Railway Board of Directors in February 1866, and on the signing of the Charter of Incorporation of the Borough of Barrow-in-Furness on 13th June 1867, he became the town's first Mayor.

The same month saw the opening for passenger traffic of the Furness and Midland Joint Line between Wennington Junction and Carnforth Furness and Midland Junction. In spite of their lack of enthusiasm, the Midland had been held to their agreement on through traffic to Belfast and the Isle of Man. The FR, the MR and James Little and Company, shipping agents of Glasgow, were the three partners in the Barrow Steam Navigation Company formed in 1867. Bradshaw's timetable for July announced *Daily Express Service to the Isle of Man via the New Barrow Route* in the Barrow Steam Navigation Company's *PS Herald*. A Midland express left Leeds at 10.00 a.m. and ran to Piel, arriving in time for the 2.00 p.m. boat for Douglas.

Passengers in the up direction arrived at Piel at 1.15 p.m. and changed at Barrow. This service ran only during the summer season and finished on 1st October.

Even more significant was the eloquent announcement in the September Bradshaw:
BELFAST, BY THE NEW & SHORT SEA ROUTE VIA BARROW

The capacious new Docks of Barrow, situated within the Ancient Harbour of Piel, under the shelter of Walney Island, being now open for traffic, the swift, powerful, first class paddle steamships Roe, Shelburne, *and* Talbot *will now commence in connection with through trains on the Midland and Furness Railways.*

Passengers took the 11.30 a.m. Midland express from London, Kings Cross and changed at Leeds into the 5.40 p.m. for Piel Pier, arriving at 9.00 p.m. The time of 3 hours 20 minutes for the run from Leeds to Piel compares very favourably with the fastest time in 1955 of 3 hours 17 minutes from Leeds to Barrow. Only in recent years have timings significantly improved, and in the summer of 2000 the fastest time was 2 hours 36 minutes, travelling by the 2.16 p.m. departure from Leeds and arriving in Barrow at 4.52 p.m. after a change at Carnforth.

The opening of the new service was marred by an unfortunate circumstance. On 3rd May it occurred to the Board that Piel Pier, then more than 20 years old, had better be checked over before the new passenger traffic commenced. Messrs McClean and Stileman carried out an extensive examination of the pier, and on 11th July reported that it was unfit for steamboat traffic. The cost of making it serviceable was found to be nearly equal to that of reconstructing it. Tenders for the latter work were immediately invited, and the contract was given to Messrs Lander and Mellanby with instructions to commence the work at once.

Devonshire Dock east side, c.1905. On the left is the Barrow Steam Cornmill and on the right the FR Bonded store, transit shed and goods warehouse.

(Authors collection)

The greatest event of the year was the formal opening of the Devonshire Dock on Thursday 19th September 1867 (the actual opening had been on 24th August when Fisher's schooner *W&MJ* sailed into the Dock).

The Barrow Times reported:

For a considerable time preparations had been going on in order that the docks should be opened with all possible ceremony and éclat. From an early hour in the morning special trains kept pouring into the town from all parts of the Kingdom and Barrow wore its holiday dress. About noon the members of the various Friendly Societies with children from the Sunday Schools assembled at their respective stations and, forming into processional order, marched to the Market Square, each Society and School headed by a band. In the Town Hall the Mayor and Corporation were assembled with all the elite of the town and neighbourhood. Here a congratulatory address, suitable for the occasion, was presented to His Grace the Duke of Devonshire. A beautiful illuminated address was also presented, with a gold medal, to the Mayor, Mr James Ramsden, in commemoration of the Incorporation of the Town. The procession then reformed and proceeded to the open space in Duke Street, at the bottom of Paxton Terrace. His Grace the Duke of Buccleuch formally presented to the Mayor a neat fountain, which his Grace had caused to be erected there for the use of the Town. From thence the assemblage proceeded to the Pier and there awaited the arrival of the principal guests. At 2 o'clock pm His Grace the Duke of Devonshire, His Grace the Duke of Buccleuch, Right Hon W E Gladstone, Lord F Cavendish, Sir W G Armstrong, Col. Wilson Patten, MP, Chancellor of the Duchy of Lancaster, James Ramsden Esq., Mayor, with the Mayors of other cities and towns, all wearing the insignia of their office, and a host of other notabilities embarked upon the steamer Herald, *steamed round Barrow Island and entered the Dock Basin amid a salvo of 32 pounders from Her Majesty's Gunboat* Goshawk, *moored in the Channel.*

The Dock having duly been declared open, the distinguished party next paid a visit to the Iron and Steel Works, where, under the able guidance of Mr J T Smith, the Manager, they witnessed the casting of an ingot of steel from a Bessemer Furnace and the various processes through which it passed until its conversion into a finished steel rail within the short space of half an hour.

A magnificent banquet in the large carriage shed of the Company, superbly decorated for the occasion, wound up the day's proceedings and, as the Times observed, *the guests exceeded 1,100 in number and composed perhaps the most complete representative assembly of trading and railway interests in all parts of the Kingdom which has ever been assembled in England.*

Other events of the year were an agreement with the Post Office for the carriage of mails between Carnforth, Barrow and Millom and the letting of the Duddon Viaduct contract to Messrs P D Bennett and Company for £29,736. A sad occurrence was the exchange of the *Helvellyn* and £8,200 for *Walney*, a new steam tug for use in the dock and on the Fleetwood service.

The year ended with the FR Directors feeling not a little anxious. A depression in the iron trade had set in during the last few months of the year, and everyone feared that the prosperity of the 1860s was over. The dividend fell to 8% at the year-end and, as there seemed no prospect of a change for the better, the Directors decided they would have to reduce capital expenditure to a minimum. Reluctantly, they postponed the Duddon Viaduct and abandoned the Park Loop Line project in favour of the Piel Pier reconstruction, the branch to Newby Bridge and improvements at Barrow and Piel Channel. The new Piel Pier was completed in February 1868, and was on a higher level so that trains could run onto it. The main pier was 810 feet long

Devonshire Bridge Signal box, *c.1962. Behind is the tower of the hydraulic engine house, with the original Harbour Office to the left.*
(Author MAA 40)

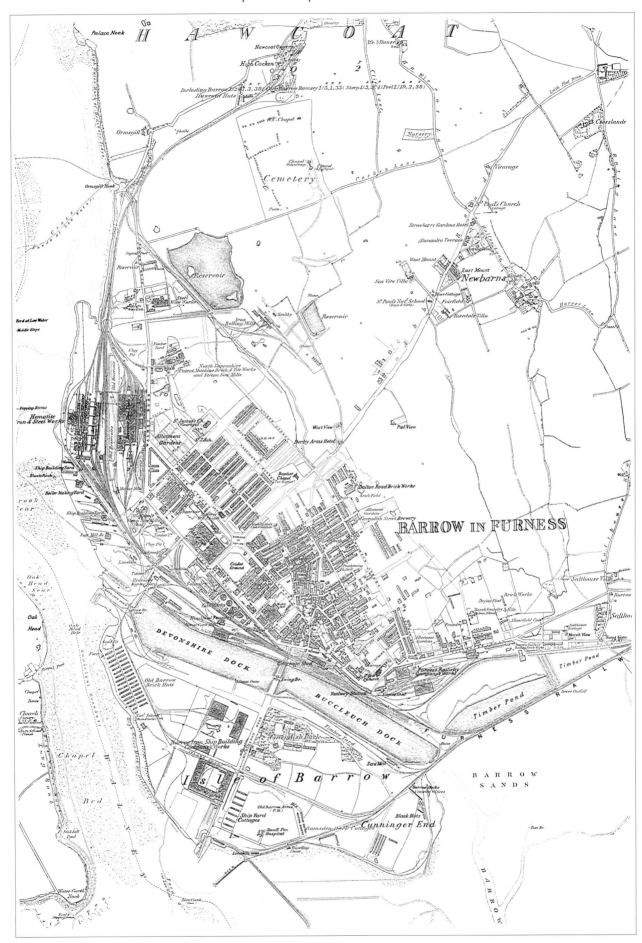

Barrow in 1873

(Ordnance Survey, Crown Copyright reserved.)

Hindpool South, 1959. View of the signalbox and Ironworks. The branch to Ironworks Road is shown in the bottom left. This siding was extended to the Devonshire Bridge line in 1916 to allow direct running between Burnip and MacDougall's oil and grease works and Vickers shell shop. (Author MAA 48)

and had two steamer landings, an upper for high tide and a lower for low tide. A small railway station with a platform one-third covered was placed halfway along this part of the pier. There was also a transverse pier 300 feet long with two steam cranes and a line of rails connected to the main line by a turntable. Twelve cottages were built on Roa Island for the railway staff there.

Other works completed at this time were a subway under the line at Hindpool at a cost of £3,000, and £10,000 worth of roads and sidings on Barrow Island. The Island was connected to the mainland by a branch from Hindpool, and this single line passed over a hydraulically operated drawbridge on the north side of the caisson between the Tidal Basin and the Dock. One siding was built along the western side of the dock and another through the middle of the Island on the site of the later Bridge Road sidings between Ferry Road and Bridge Road.

Another work carried on in 1868 was the construction of the Salthouse Embankment. This ran from Salthouse to Barrow Island and enclosed the Timber Pond and the Buccleuch Dock. In 1871 a second embankment was built from this to the south-east end of the Railway Pier. On completion of both embankments a double set of rails were laid on them and the main line from Salthouse was diverted onto the new route. The track on the old embankment was taken up between Salthouse and the railway works and engine shed. As the Roose road was not yet completed a new level crossing was made on the new main line at Salthouse, at a point a few yards east of the present Junction Ground Frame. After the diversion of the main line had been completed, the cut for the Abbey Beck was made along the north side of the old embankment from Roose to the old crossing, where a section of the embankment was removed to let the stream flow into the Timber Pond.

Barrow Steelworks, c.1895.
The Rail Rolling Mill.
(From North Lonsdale Magazine, Geoff Holme collection)

Salthouse, 1955. In about 1868 the Abbey Beck had to be diverted because of the building of the Salthouse Embankment and a bridge carried the road from the Sandgate Hotel to the sands. This bridge was superseded by the present structure in about 1880 to improve road access to the paper mills. In the left background is the 1919 gas works. *(Author MAC 19)*

Near the site of the old Salthouse crossing a narrow, decorative stone and iron bridge was laid across the cut to carry the road. This bridge survived until the 1950s, although it had been long superseded by the much wider structure now in use, which was built later at the point where the cut emptied into the Timber Pond. The old embankment can still be clearly seen as it runs behind the houses at the top of Salthouse Road. Its Barrow end was obliterated by the building of Claye's Carriage and Wagon Works in the early 1870s. Yet another line built in 1868 was a tramway from Roose up to Yarlside Iron Mine. Until around 1873, when the branch was rebuilt as a standard gauge siding, the line was a patent narrow gauge system by J B Fell running up to the mine from a loading dock a quarter of a mile from Roose.

Barrow Ironworks, c.1902, viewed from North Scale. The ancient ford and footbridge from Cocken to North Scale is in the foreground. In the right background are the factories on Ironworks Road. *(Maud Tranter collection, Dock Museum, Barrow)*

LOCAL RAILWAY TIME TABLE, FROM JULY 1, 1876.

UP.	WEEK DAYS.											SUNDAYS.					
	a.m.	a.m.	a.m.	a.m.	p.m.	noon	p.m.	p.m.	p.m.	p.m	p.m.	a.m.	a.m	p.m	p.m.		
Whitehaven (dep)	....	....	6 45	9 40	....	12 0	....	....	....	4 0	6 0	....	....	....	....	....	....
Millom (Holborn Hill)	...	....	8 10	1055	....	1 13	....	2 10	....	5 18	7 22	....	8 33	....	6 43	....	....
Foxfield Junction arr	....	....	8 27	1110	....	1 24	....	2 20	....	5 28	7 35	....	8 45	....	6 55	....	....
Coniston Lake (depart)	....	....	8 0	1040	....	1250	....	....	2 5	4 50	7 0	....	8 15	....	6 25	....	....
Foxfield Junction „	....	....	8 35	1115	....	1 29	....	2 20	....	5 30	7 38	....	8 50	....	7 0	....	....
Kirkby	...	....	8 41	1121	....	1 35	....	2 25	....	5 36	7 43	....	8 55	....	7 5	....	....
Askam	....	....	8 49	1129	....	1 43	....	2 35	....	5 44	7 52	....	9 8	....	7 18	....	....
Dalton	....	....	9 0	1140	....	1 53	....	2 50	....	5 55	8 3	....	9 18	....	7 28	....	....
Barrow Branch.																	
Furness Ab. arr.	...	....	9 25	1150	....	2 5	....	2 55	2 55	6 5	8 15	..	9 25	....	7 35	....	....
Roose ...... „	....	.	9 30	12 0	....	2 15	....	3 5	3 5	6 15	8 25	....	9 35	....	7 45	....	...
Barrow .... „	....	....	9 35	12 5	....	2 20	....	3 10	3 10	6 20	8 30	....	9 40	....	7 50	....	....
	am.	a.m	a.m.	a.m.	p.m.	p.m.	p.m.		p.m.	p.m.	p.m.	a.m.	a.m	p.m.	p.m.		....
Barrow ..depart	6 0	6 15	8 45	1125	1 15	1 40	2 50		4 30	5 45	7 50	6 45	9 0	4 45	7 10	....	....
Roose .... „	6 5	....	8 50	1130	1 20	....	2 55		....	5 50	7 55	6 50	9 5	4 50	7 15	....	....
Furness Abbey „	6 10	6 23	8 55	1135	1 25	1 48	3 0		4 38	5 55	8 0	6 55	9 10	4 55	7 20	....	....
Dalton .... „	6 15	6 28	9 10	1145	1 30	1 58	3 5		....	6 0	8 8	7 5	9 20	5 0	7 30		....
Lindal .... „	6 20	....	9 15	1150	1 35	....	3 10		....	6 5	8 13	7 10	9 25	5 5	7 35	....	....
Ulverston ....arrive	6 30	6 40	9 25	12 0	1 45	2 10	3 20		4 50	6 15	8 23	7 20	9 35	5 15	7 50	....	....
Windermere Branch.																	
Ulverston depart	....	....	9 30	1210	1 55	3 25	3 25		4 55	6 45	8 35	....	9 45	5 20	....	....	....
Greenodd	....	....	9 36	1216	2 1	3 31	3 31		5 1	6 51	8 41	....	9 51	5 26	....	....	....
Haverthwaite	....	....	9 42	1222	2 7	3 37	3 37		5 7	6 57	8 47	....	9 58	5 32	....	....	....
Lake Side, arrive	....	....	9 55	1235	2 20	3 50	3 50		5 20	7 10	9 0	....	1010	5 45	....	....	....
Bowness „	....	....	1050	3 15	3 15	5 0	5 0		6 15	8 0	....	....	....	....	....	....	....
Ambleside „	....	....	1120	3 45	3 45	5 30	5 30		6 45	8 30	...	....	....	....	....	....	....
Ambleside, dep	....	....	....	10 0	1140	1140	1 10		1 10	3 50	6 30	....	....	....	....	....	....
Bowness „	....	....	....	1030	1210	1210	1 40		1 40	4 20	6 50	....	....	....	....	....	....
Lake Side „	....	....	8 35	1130	1 15	1 15	2 50		4 10	5 25	7 55	....	....	4 45	....	....	....
Haverthwaite „	....	....	8 42	1137	1 22	1 22	2 57		4 17	5 32	8 2	....	....	4 52	....	....	....
Greenodd „	....	....	8 50	1145	1 30	1 30	3 5		4 25	5 40	8 10	....	....	5 0	....	....	....
Ulverston, arrive	....	....	9 0	1155	1 40	1 40	3 15		4 35	5 50	8 20	....	....	5 10	....	....	....
Ulverston depart	6 43		9 39	12 5	1 30	2 13	3 25		4 53	6 18	8 25	7 20	9 40	5 15	....	....	....
Cark and Cartmel „	6 58		9 45	1220	2 5	....	3 40		....	6 30	8 38	7 35	9 55	5 30	....	....	....
Kents Bank .... „	7 5		9 52	1227	2 12	....	3 47		....	6 35	8 44	7 42	10 2	5 37	....	....	....
Grange-over-Sands	7 10		9 57	1235	2 20	2 35	3 52		5 15	6 40	8 50	7 47	1010	5 45	....	....	....
Arnside .... „	7 17		10 4	1242	2 27	....	4 0		....	6 47	8 56	7 54	1017	5 52	....	....	....
Silverdale.. ...	7 25		1012	1250	2 35	....	4 8		....	6 55	9 4	8 2	1025	6 0	....	....	....
Carnforth, (F & M.) arr	7 35		1025	....	2 45	3 0	....		....	....	....	8 10	....	6 13	....	....	....
„ (L. & N.W.) „	7 40		1030	1 5	2 50	3 5	4 25		5 40	7 10	9 20	8 15	1010	6 15	....	....	....
Preston ......Arrive	8 35		1133	2 40	....	4 10	6 5		6 45	8 20	1020	....	....	8 15	....	....	....
Manchester L&Y „	10 0		....	5 5	....	5 20	8 0		8 30	1015	1130	....	....	10 0	....	....	....
„ L&NW „	1015		1 0	....	....	6 5	8 5		8 5	9 50	1130	....	....	1248	....	....	...
L'pool, Lime-st „	1030		1 5	5 35	....	5 35	8 10		8 10	9 50	1145	....	....	1145	....	....	..
„ Exchange-st „	1010		1255	4 40	....	5 15	7 45		9 15	10 0	....	....	....	1010	....	....	....
Birmingham .... „	1230		3 40	6 25	....	8 27	1110		1110	2 30	2 30	....	....	2 30	....	....	....
London, Euston „	3 0		5 40	8 30	....	9 45	....		....	5 30	5 30	....	....	5 30	....	....	....

DOWN	WEEK DAYS.												SUNDAYS.				
	p.m.	a.m	a.m.	a.m.	a.m.	a.m	a.m.	a m	a.m.	a.m.	a.m	a.m.	p.m.	a.m.	a.m.	p.m.	a.m.
London, Euston..dep.	9 0	....	....	....	....	5 15	7 15	7 15	9 0	1010	11 0	12 0	9 0	....	....	....	10 0
Birmingham .... „	1030	....	....	....	...	7 25	8 50	8 50	11 0	1140	1220	2 10	1030	....	....	....	1 5
Liverpool Lime-st „	1235	....	....	....	6 0	9 30	1050	....	1 30	2 0	3 50	4 25	1235	....	....	....	3 45
„ Exchange-st „	....	....	....	....	6 25	9 0	1030	1030	1 25	2 45	4 10	4 15	....	....	....	....	1 0
Manchester L & Y „	....	....	....	....	6 10	9 50	11 0	11 0	1 25	2 35	4 25	4 50	....	....	....	....	1 0
„ L & N W „	1 0	....	....	....	6 0	9 25	11 0	11 0	1 30	2 0	3 55	4 20	1 0	....	....	....	...
Preston .... „	2 35	....	....	6 0	8 5	11 5	1230	1245	2 55	3 50	5 15	6 10	2 35	....	8 20	....	6 55
	a.m	a.m.	a.m.	a.m.	a.m.	a m.	p.m.	p.m.	p.m.	p.m.	p.m.	p.m.	a.m.	a.m.	a.m.	p.m.	p.m
Carnforth .. Depart	4 40	....	8 10	9 50	12 0	1230	1 30	2 30	4 0	5 0	6 5	7 30	4 40	....	9 45	....	7 30
(F. & M. Junct.) „	....	....	....	9 53	....	1235	....	....	....	5 5	....	....	....	....	9 47	....	7 32
Silverdale........ „	....	....	8 30	10 0	....	....	...	2 40	....	5 12	....	7 40	....	....	9 55	....	7 40
Arnside .... „	....	....	8 27	10 7	....	....	....	2 47	....	5 19	....	7 47	...	....	10 2	....	7 47
Grange over-Sands „	5 0	....	8 35	1015	1220	1255	1 50	2 55	4 25	5 25	6 20	7 55	5 0	....	1010	....	7 55
Kents Bank .. ... „	....	...	8 42	1020	....	....	....	3 2	....	5 32	....	8 6	....	....	1017	....	8 0
Cark and Cartmel..	....	....	8 51	1030	....	....	....	3 10	....	5 40	....	8 5	....	....	1025	....	8 10
Ulverston .. Arrive	5 21	....	9 5	1015	1240	1 15	2 10	3 25	4 45	5 55	6 40	8 20	5 20	....	1040	....	8 30
Windermere Branch.																	
Ulverston Depart	....	....	9 30	1055		1 55		3 25	4 55		6 45	8 35	....	....	1050	....	....
Greenodd .... „	....	....	9 36	11 1		2 1		3 31	5 1		6 51	8 41	....	....	1056	....	....
Haverthwaite „	....	....	9 42	11 7		2 7		3 37	5 7		6 57	8 47	....	....	11 2	....	....
Lake Side, W. Arr.	....	....	9 55	1120		2 20		3 50	5 20		7 10	9 0	....	..	1115	....	....
Bowness .. „	....	....	1050	1230		3 15		5 0	6 15		8 0		....	....			
Ambleside „	....	....	1120	1 0		3 45		5 30	6 45		8 30		....	....	....	....	....
Ambleside Dep	....	....	....	8 20	10 0		1140	1 10	1 10	3 50	....	6 30	....	....	....	....	....
Bowness .. „	....	....	....	9 0	1030		1210	1 40	1 40	4 20	....	6 50	....	....	....	....	....
Lake Side, W. „	....	....	8 35	1010	1130		1 15	2 50	4 10	5 25	....	7 55	....	....	1015	6 0	...
Haverthwaite „	....	....	8 42	1017	1137		1 22	2 57	4 17	5 32	....	8 2	....	....	1022	6 7	....
Greenodd .... „	....	....	8 50	1025	1145		1 30	3 5	4 25	5 40	....	8 10	....	....	1030	6 15	....
Ulverston	....	....	9 0	1035	1155		1 40	3 15	4 35	5 50	....	8 20	....	....	1040	6 25	....
Ulverston .. Depart	5 20	7 0	9 5	1050	1243	1 18	2 13	3 25	4 50	6 0	6 40	8 25	5 20	8 20	1040	6 25	8 30
Lindal .... „	....	7 10	9 15	11 0	....	....	....	3 35	....	6 10	....	8 35	....	8 30	1050	6 35	8 40
Dalton ....Arr	5 35	7 15	9 20	11 5	....	....	2 20	3 40	5 2	6 15	....	8 40	5 35	8 35	1055	6 45	8 45
Barrow Branch																	
Furness Ab'y „	5 45	7 20	9 25	1115	1255	1 35	2 25	3 45	5 10	6 20	7 0	8 45	5 45	8 40	11 0	6 5[illegible]	8 50
Roose ...... „	....	7 30	9 30	1125	....	....	....	3 55	....	6 25	....	8 55	....	8 45	11 5	6 5[illegible]	8 55
Barrow .... „	5 55	7 35	9 35	1130	1 10	2 20	2 40	4 0	5 20	6 30	7 15	9 0	5 55	8 50	1110	7 0	9 0
Barrow Depart	5 20	7 0	....	1045	1250	....	2 50	....	4 45	6 50		....	5 20	8 20	....	6 25	....
Roose ...... „	....	7 5	....	1050	....	....	2 25	....	....	6 55		....	....	8 25	....	6 30	....
Furness Ab'y Dep.	....	7 10	....	1055	1 0	....	3 10	....	4 53	7 5		....	....	8 30	....	6 35	....
Dalton	5 35	7 20	....	1110	1 5	....	....	....	5 0	....		....	5 35	8 35	....	6 40	....
Askam .... „	....	7 30	....	1120	1 15	....	3 20	....	5 18	7 16		....	....	8 45	....	6 50	....
Kirkby .. .. „	....	7 38	....	1128	1 23	....	....	....	5 26	7 23		....	....	8 55	....	7 5	....
Foxfield Junction Arr.	5 55	7 41	....	1134	1 30	....	....	....	5 32	7 20		....	5 55	9 0	....	7 15	....
Coniston Lake ..Arr	....	9 15	....	1215	1 55	....	4 0	....	6 5	8 10		....	....	9 30	....	7 50	....
Coniston Lake ..Dep	....	....	....	1040	1250	....	....	....	4 50	7 0		....	....	8 15	....	6 25	....
Foxfield Junct.	5 55	7 45	....	1139	1 30	....	....	....	5 37	7 29		....	5 55	9 5	....	7 20	....
Millom (Holborn Hill)	6 5	7 57	....	1150	1 40	....	....	....	5 47	7 40		....	6 5	9 17	....	7 32	....
Whitehaven	7 15	9 20	....	1 10	....	....	....	....	7 0	9 0		....	....	....	....	....	....

Furness Railway Time Table, *from The Barrow Herald, 29th November 1876.* *(Author's collection)*

Yarlside, c.1958. 2-8-0 48654 hauls a Barrow to Carnforth freight. In the background is the Yarlside mine with its large subsidence, below which a section of the Yarlside branch can be seen. (Author MAA 1)

During 1868 the depression worsened and traffic fell off. At the end of October the attention of the Directors was drawn to the fact that the Duddon Crossing Powers lapsed on 29th June of the following year, so they determined to re-examine the economy of the scheme, and drew up the following analysis:

5% on cost of Viaduct @ £85,000	£4250
Loss on mileage rate by shorter route	£5500
Extra maintenance	£10400
Less saving in running expense	£750
Total deficit	£9650

Equivalent extra through tonnage per annum 150,000 tons.

The saving in running expense was so small because of the necessity of keeping open the old route for Coniston traffic.

The Directors resolved that *the Duddon Crossing be abandoned*, although a large sum had already been spent on the works at Askam. A Bill was deposited for the abandonment of the Park Loop and the Duddon Crossing, receiving Royal Assent after a clause had been added to the effect that tolls for traffic starting at Ireleth and ending at Millom were to be based on the direct crossing mileage.

1869 saw the letting of the contract for the new Graving Dock, now the site of the Dock Museum, which was to be built next to the Devonshire Dock entrance basin. In 1870 a new steamer pier was built on the west shore of Barrow Island connected to the main line by a branch railway from Buccleuch Junction on the Salthouse embankment. The line ran over the southern tip of Barrow Island and was connected to the two lines already on the island. This branch did not become important until Ramsden Dock had been completed, when it was used by the Midland Boat Trains to and from Ramsden Dock Station.

In the latter part of 1868 borings had been carried out at Piel Bar, which formed an obstruction in the channel. Contrary to popular belief, the bar was found to consist of sand and gravel rather than boulders, and so could easily be dredged. After some delay a dredger was bought and this commenced operations in 1870.

By 1870 the new steamer services were well established. On the opening of the second season in June 1868, the Belfast Boat Train had earlier departures at 9.10 a.m. from Kings Cross and 3.50 p.m. from Leeds, arriving at Piel at 7.00 p.m. Return facilities had been provided, passengers leaving Piel at 7.00 a.m., and arriving at Kings Cross at 3.50 p.m., after changing at Leeds. In 1869, St Pancras Station being opened, the train left there at 9.00 a.m., but took longer over the Leeds to Piel part of the run. The Fleetwood service did not appear in the 1869 tables, being abandoned at the end of the 1868 season.

The timetable showed the Boat Trains calling at Carnforth F and M Junction Station, then running to Furness Abbey where they divided into Piel and Barrow portions. One hour and ten minutes was spent over the run from Carnforth to Barrow. Another notable train was the Down Mail which commenced in September 1869. This left Carnforth at 4.30 a.m. and arrived in Whitehaven at 7.00 a.m., stops being made at Ulverston and Foxfield. This train, which in its last years ran as the 01.05 Postal from Huddersfield to Workington, continued in service until 28 September 1991. On its last journeys it was still timetabled to leave Carnforth at 04.30, arriving at Whitehaven at 06.47 despite running over the 8-mile longer route via Barrow. The train then ran as a parcels train to Workington where it was stabled until its return journey.

Devonshire Bridge box, *7th July 1968, on the single line between Cornmill Crossing and Bridge Road sidings on Barrow Island. The bridge was shared between road and rail traffic. Before a train could be signalled, wheel-operated gates had to close the road here and at Walney Ferry box on the west side of the bridge. This box dated from 1888 and after closure in 1972 was transferred to the miniature railway in Barrow Park.* *(Author MAA 730)*

Devonshire Dock bridge, *c.1970, looking east over the bridge. This was originally a single span, hydraulic lifting bridge dating from about 1867. In 1916 it had to be fixed due to corrosion and finally replaced by this structure still to be seen inside the BAE Systems Devonshire Dock Hall compound. By this time ships entered the docks system by the Ramsden Dock gates.* *(Ken Norman)*

From the Incorporation of the Borough in 1867, the town continued to expand at great speed. The population, which was about 11,000 at that time, had increased to 28,000 in 1872 and by 1875 had grown to 35,000. Although houses were built by William Gradwell at a tremendous rate he could not keep up with demand, and in 1873 the Shipbuilding Company had to erect a temporary estate of wooden huts on the North Western corner of Barrow Island to house its employees. These were condemned as early as 1877, having been replaced by the Devonshire Buildings, built to the design of the FR Architects Paley & Austin, on Michaelson and Ramsden Dock Roads, with finance being provided by the Duke of Devonshire.

The Managers of both the Railway and the Shipyard were not forgotten, and Devonshire in his diary for 22nd March 1870 records: *We walked over Barrow Island and Ramsden explained his ideas as to the site of the shipbuilding yard and also to that for a better class of houses which seem to be much required.* The Barrow Times of 25th February 1871 reported that *a number of substantial villas are being erected.* This was to be Cavendish Park, constructed off Michaelson Road west of the Buccleuch Dock Road. They were semi-detached and built of sandstone and there were tennis courts within the private estate. Amongst the first residents were the Furness Railway Accountant, Resident Engineer, Harbour Master, Dock Contract Manager, Channel Dredging Manager and Barrow Steam Navigation Company Manager. The Shipbuilding Company Manager and the Vicar of St. John's Church also lived on the estate. In 1939 Cavendish Park was sold to Vickers, and in the early 1950s the north part including the lodge was demolished to make

way for an engineering workshop which, after being used to build Sulzer engines for British Railways diesel locomotives, is currently occupied by the Royal Ordinance. Only two pairs of villas still stand.

More significant from the railway point of view was the introduction of many new commercial enterprises, all of which had rail sidings, and by 1867 several factories were already in operation on the Hindpool Estate. As early as 1855 William Gradwell had moved his timber yard from the original site at Barrow Pier, and his new Hindpool Sawmills were connected to the Hawcoat Branch by a siding which continued to be known as Gradwell's Siding many years after the Gradwell business had moved away. This area is now occupied by Hollywood Park retail development. In 1865 William Ashburner moved his shipbuilding and repair yard from its Devonshire Dock site to the shore at Hindpool. His new yard was reached by a siding which crossed the Ironworks road, leaving the Hawcoat Branch at the south end of the Ironworks Sidings where a signal box named Hindpool South had been built. A curve connected this siding with the Barrow Island branch just before it crossed Devonshire Dock bridge, giving direct access between the factories in Ironworks Road and Barrow Island. The siding was still in use in the 1950s to reach the works of Messrs Little and Angus, but the curve, though still existing, was unused. In 1866 Messrs Westray and Forster, later Westray and Copeland, opened their Iron Foundry at the southern end of the estate, and this operated as Caird's Foundry until closure in the late 1980s. After demolition in 1989/90, the site is now occupied by the Cornerhouse Park retail development.

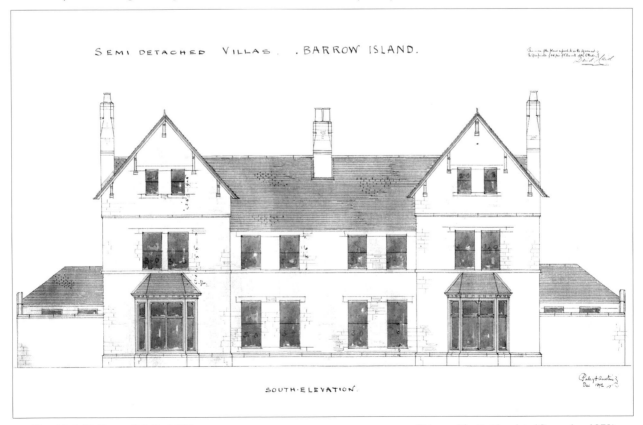

Nos 11 & 12 Cavendish Park Villas.   *(Paley and Austin plan dated December 1872)*

Cornmill Crossing, *c.1895. At the north end of Barrow Yard, the box shown here was opened in 1882 and subsequently replaced c.1919. The later box was closed in 1972 after the Barrow Yard lines were removed with the exception of a single line from Salthouse Junction to the Shipyard gates at Walney Ferry. The Barrow Steam Cornmill is on the right.* (From North Lonsdale Magazine, Geoff Holme collection)

The year 1870 saw the promotion of two more important companies which established their works on the Hindpool Estate, and both were Ramsden-Devonshire projects. The Barrow Flax and Jute Company's works was built across Hindpool Road from the Westray and Forster's Foundry, the building being completed in 1872, and was reached by a siding which crossed Hindpool Road. The second works, built in connection with the existing grain warehouses on the east side of the dock, was the Barrow Steam Cornmill Company, sold in 1880 to Messrs Walmsley and Smith Ltd. At the north end of the estate a wire-works, completed in October 1870, was built adjacent to the steelworks by Messrs Cooke and Swinnerton, whilst the Walney Road Brickworks, started in 1873 and completed in 1876, was built on a site now occupied by the Asda Superstore.

The most important works on the Hindpool Estate was that of Barrow Haematite Steel Company. From the merger in 1866 of the iron and steel works, the plant expanded rapidly and many miles of sidings were put in. The ironworks and the steelworks were on either side of the Hawcoat branch, and sidings from each works joined the branch at Hindpool South and Hindpool North signalboxes.

Walney Road Brickworks, *c.1895. This was one of a number of industrial sites served by sidings from the Hawcoat Branch. (From Sea Ports of the Furness Railway, Geoff Holme collection)*

David Caird's Foundry, *Hindpool Road, one of the factories with its own locomotives. The Manning Wardle 0-4-0 tank seen here was built in 1885, came second hand to Barrow in 1923 and was in use until the 1940s. Further steam and diesel locomotives were used on this site until the BR connection was severed in the early 1980s. The site is now occupied by the Cornerhouse Park retail development.*
(Cumbria Record Office & Local Studies Library, Barrow - David Caird collection BDP/68/6)

Cornmill Crossing, *12th August 1902. Furness Railway 0-4-0 No.28 was built by Sharp Stewart in 1866 and withdrawn in 1918. Surviving long after six of her sisters had been sold to the the Barrow Steelworks and converted to tank engines, No.28 is seen shunting Cornmill Sidings. One of her sold sisters, No. 20, has survived and has been rebuilt to her original Victorian condition.*
(LCGB Ken Nunn collection)

Buccleuch Dock. The south west end was occupied by the timber yard of Price, Potter and Walker, later Crossfields, until a southern extension of the Vickers shipyard was built. In the background, the High Level Bridge, Barrow Town Hall and Barrow Yard can be seen. The German manufactured crane shown in the photograph was demolished by enemy action in May 1941.
(Wyn Anderson Collection)

Around 1870 the BHS Company built a small steel rolling mill at the top end of the present Ainslie Street, and this extension to the Steel Works was significant because it influenced the future layout of the Furness Railway main line. Direct access by rail to the new mill was prevented by the position of the wire-works, and, in order to provide a railway connection, it was necessary to build a siding some three-quarters of a mile in length, running south east from the Hawcoat Branch. When the Barrow Loop was projected in 1871, it was obvious that the cheapest course was to make this siding the north end of the loop, and thus the position of the present Station was determined.

About this time, Barrow Island began to develop as an industrial centre. William Gradwell took over the north-west side of Devonshire Dock as a timber storage yard, which was used for the same purpose by Messrs Burt, Boulton and Heywood Ltd. until the 1970s. In 1868 a second firm of timber importers, Messrs Price, Potter and Walker, established a timber yard and sawmill on the north-east side of the Dock, and this was moved to the south-west side of Buccleuch Dock on Barrow Island in 1873. By far the most important works on Barrow Island was the Barrow Shipbuilding Company, whose first Directors Meeting was held at Ramsden's home, Abbot's Wood, on

28th January 1871. Estimated to cost £92,000 the works, completed in 1872, occupied the land between the western side of Devonshire Dock and the west shore of the island. The complex was divided into two parts by the Barrow Island Loop Line on Island Road (now Bridge Road), the western half being the slipways and the eastern the engineering and fitting shops. The works was connected to the existing line of railway on the island.

The third area of industrial development was Salthouse Marsh, where a foundry had been opened in 1860, which by 1870 was owned by Joseph Briggs. This foundry, which was across Salthouse Road from the old main line, was reached by a siding built in 1874 which must have crossed this road on the level, but no sign of this or the foundry it served now remains except the name of the nearby Foundry Street.

In 1870 S J Claye of the Manor Works, Long Eaton, Derbyshire bought 7 acres of land on Salthouse Marsh on which he built carriage and wagon works, with the Furness Railway as a principal customer, a large contract being instrumental in attracting him to Barrow. Although the enterprise was small initially, with many metal components coming from Long Eaton, by 1873 the works were complete and in full production. Following expansion the works were soon capable of holding 100 carriages at a time.

Devonshire Dock, c.1895, showing Gradwell's timber wharf. In the foreground is the caisson which separated Devonshire Dock from its tidal basin. In front of the caisson can be seen part of the combined rail & road lifting bridge.
(From Sea Ports of the Furness Railway, Geoff Holme collection)

Barrow Jute Works, *c.1895, one of the enterprises of the FR directors. When opened in 1872, it was served by a siding which crossed Hindpool Road. It closed in the 1920s and, when demolished, the site was occupied by Lakeland Laundries, Barrow Bus Depot and the John Winnerah Institute. Recently the site has been redeveloped as a retail park. In the foreground is the Parade Ground, subsequently built over.* *(Geoff Holme collection)*

Barrow Yard, *North end from High Level Bridge, c.1900, with the FR warehouse and Barrow Cornmill in the background. In the left foreground FR No.16, purchased in 1861, is taking water. On the right is Waddingtons foundry.* *(George Taylor collection)*

Ship Street, *Devonshire Buildings, Barrow Island, c.1910. This extensive estate was built with funds provided by the FR chairman, the 7th Duke of Devonshire, to provide much needed accommodation for the expanding workforce of Barrow industry in the early 1870s. The frontage onto Michaelson Road, designed by Paley and Austin, is dressed with sandstone. The estate remains in use.*
(Ken Norman collection)

Barrow Shipyard, *c.1880. An artist's impression by G H Andrews of a ship being launched into Walney Channel from one of the slipways of the Barrow Shipbuilding Company. In the background are the chimneys of the Iron and Steel Works.*   *(Dock Museum, Barrow)*

By the end of 1869 the depression was over and traffic and profit began to rise steadily, so that in 1871 the Furness Railway was able to carry on with Ramsden's expansion plans. Two major development schemes were proposed in 1871. The first of these was conceived on an ambitious scale and concerned an increase in the dock accommodation at Barrow. The Buccleuch Dock was to be completed, and then an embankment would be constructed between Ramsey Island and the mainland at Parrock Hall, to create another dock, the Ramsden, connected with the existing dock system by a cut in the Salthouse Embankment. The Channel Pier branch would be carried on a swing bridge over this cut. There was an arrangement whereby ships of the Anchor Line were to ply between Barrow and America on completion of the new dock. A similar scheme was sought with the Ocean Steamship Company in 1872, and in February of that year Ramsden proposed that the new docks should be built out to a point beyond Piel Pier if that Company would agree to move its traffic to Barrow. This latter proposal did not materialise (fortunately in view of later shareholder criticism of capital expenditure on the docks), and the first plan was settled on.

The second scheme was to ease the then very heavy ore traffic between Lindal and Hindpool Works. The engineer, F C Stileman (J R McClean having retired in 1869), suggested two loop lines which together would provide an alternative route between these two points. The first, named the 'Gleaston Loop', left the main line east of Lindal, curved southwards to Little Urswick and Gleaston where it turned south-west, passing north of Leece before reaching Salthouse. Here it was to pass over the Piel branch before rejoining the main line. From this same junction the second, or 'Barrow Loop', was to run directly north-west to join the Hawcoat Branch at Cocken using an existing siding at its Cocken end. A branch from the Gleaston Loop to the new iron mines at Stank was also planned.

A Bill for these works was deposited later in 1871. The Bill also included renewal of the powers to stop up the Salthouse and Roosecote Crossings, as the time limit of the 1866 Act had expired, and the Salthouse Crossing was in a different location, being on the newer Salthouse Embankment. The increase in capital to be authorised in this Bill was the colossal sum of £1,300,000, equal to half the entire existing Capital. The Bill became law on 18th July 1872, but, because of a more ambitious Bardsea Loop plan, the Gleaston Loop Scheme was withdrawn at the last minute except for the line between Salthouse and Stank mines, which was to be a single mineral line. This Bardsea Loop would have been a new main line to Barrow avoiding the steep climb to Lindal, and would have run from Plumpton Junction to Bardsea along the route later followed by the Bardsea branch, built from Plumpton Junction as far as Conishead Priory in 1883. From Bardsea the line would have followed the sea shore as far as Baycliffe where the route turned inland, and after passing

Stank Mine, 1879. Iron ore was discovered at Stank in 1870 while prospecting for coal. The branch from Salthouse Junction was opened in 1873. Standing in the sidings is 0-4-0 No.16 dating from 1861, a larger version of No.3 now preserved in the National Railway Museum at York. (photo by Hargreaves, Dalton, supplied by Jon Wilkinson, with acknowledgments to the late Mrs Edna Millard)

Furness Railway Floating Dock *seen in the Devonshire Dock. This was purchased in 1880 for £50,000 as an alternative to a more expensive second graving dock.* *(From Seaports of the Furness Railway, Geoff Holme collection)*

Newbiggin would have curved southwards of Leece to join the line of the route followed by the Stank branch from Leece Lane to Salthouse Junction. The new Roosecote Road (now Old Rampside Road) passed over this line on a bridge close to the site of Roose Hospital. This bridge allowed for double track, indicating the intention to construct a main line through route at the time of building.

The end of February 1872 saw the completion of the Buccleuch Dock, while by August the Graving Dock was in use and the various new works had been commenced. Besides the Barrow Loop and the Stank Branch, the Arnside to Hincaster Junction line was started, doubling of the Whitehaven and Furness Junction line continued, and road diversion schemes at Barrow were finished. It was also

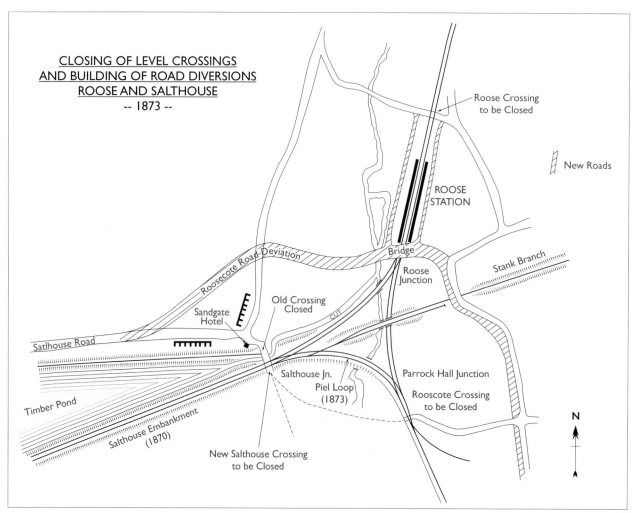

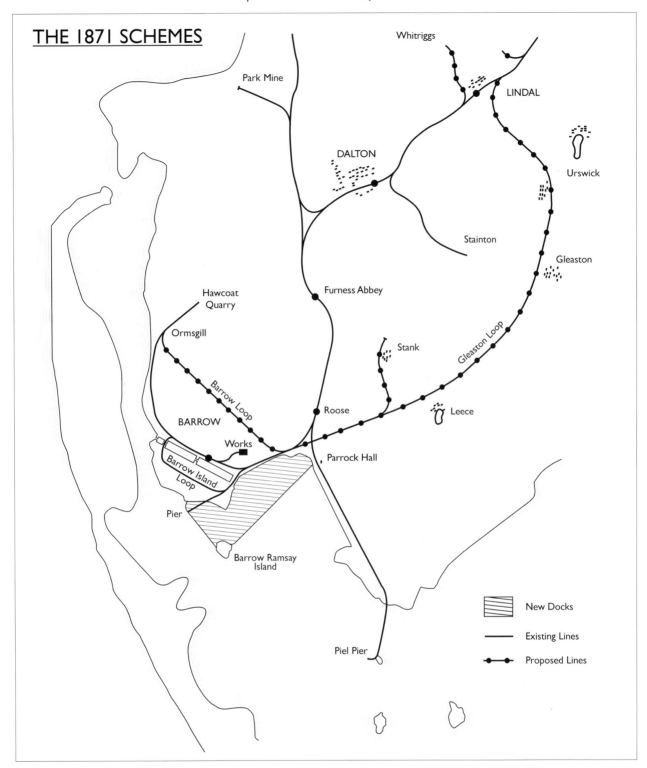

THE 1871 SCHEMES

(map labels) Whitriggs, Park Mine, LINDAL, DALTON, Urswick, Hawcoat Quarry, Stainton, Gleaston, Ormsgill, Barrow Loop, Furness Abbey, Stank, Gleaston Loop, BARROW, Roose, Leece, Works, Barrow Island Loop, Parrock Hall, Pier, Barrow Ramsay Island, New Docks, Existing Lines, Proposed Lines, Piel Pier

proposed to enlarge the station at Barrow, and to build a new carriage shed and new engine shed. The loop at Salthouse, giving direct access to the Piel Branch from Barrow, was built in this year. This connection, known as the Piel Loop, running from the Stank Branch Junction at Salthouse Junction, to Parrock Hall on the Piel Line, was not given Parliamentary sanction until the Act of 1879. Before this, the junction for the Piel Line had been moved westwards to its original site and the present double-line Roose Station built. The signal box for the Piel Line Junction (Roose Junction) was on the up side of the line, and on the west side of the newly built road bridge. The 1873 OS Map shows a double line as far as Parrock Hall.

In the first half of 1873 the Stank Branch was completed. Intended originally as the Gleaston Loop, it left the main line at a point a few yards south-west of the junction of the Salthouse Embankment with the old main line, then rose steeply to cross the Piel Branch by a bridge. Entering a short cutting the line passed under the Roosecote Road, crossed the valley on a single track embankment, and cut through the hill behind Roosecote Farm to reach the Leece Road. This was crossed by a bridge, at which point the Gleaston Loop was to have diverged. From here the line rose at 1 in 40, running through fields parallel to the Stank road, passing west of the village, crossing the road on a bridge, and terminating at Stank Mine some 300 yards north-east

Old Rampside Road Bridge *over the Stank Branch at Roose, May 1959. The bridge was built for double line when the Gleaston Loop to Lindal and later the Bardsea Loop to Plumpton were under consideration. The wagon stands at the platform for loading sand. In the foreground is a 'scotch block' to protect against a wagon running away down the bank to Salthouse Junction.* (Author MAC 25)

of the village. The length of the line was about 2 miles. As new pits were opened they were connected to the new branch by tramways, and by 1889 two had been built. The first went north-east to North Stank Mine near Newton, whilst the second left the main branch just before the bridge at Stank and curved away to the north-west to serve No. 5 and No. 8 pits. The formations of these tramways may still be seen which was just over the hill from No. 8 pit.

A sad event of 1873 was the death of John Robinson McClean. A former President of the Institution of Civil Engineers, he had been the Furness Railway Company's Engineer since the passing of the Act of Parliament in 1844, and had designed many of the Company's lines and dock works. He had retired in 1869 and his place taken by his junior partner, Mr F C Stileman.

Stank Branch *looking west, c.1969, from Old Rampside Road bridge. On the left is Barrow Gasworks.* (Author MAO 2812)

The new works were well under way when, about the middle of 1874, the wonderful prosperity, which had largely continued from 1860, came to a sudden end. An iron trade depression set in and Barrow was badly affected. The FR Directors took a large share of the responsibility and realised that they had taken on more financial commitments than was prudent. Besides their vast capital expenditure on the Furness Railway and the Dock developments, they had promoted, and had considerable interests in, the Barrow Haematite Steel Company, the Barrow Shipbuilding Company, the Barrow Flax and Jute Company, and the Barrow Steam Cornmill Company. All of these suffered badly, the Barrow Shipbuilding Company to such an extent that it came very near to collapse. Devonshire in his diary on 12th March 1877 noted: *It clearly will be necessary for me to find a great deal of money to prevent a smash.* He took the whole of the £200,000 of new share capital the Shipbuilding Company directors resolved to raise.

The railway itself, however, continued to pay its way. The dividend fell from 9.5% for 1873 to 6.5% for the years 1874-76, rising again to 8% for the second half of 1877, which in UK railway terms were excellent results.

An acute depression in 1879 sent it down to 3.5%, but it recovered to 6.5% during the early 1880s, a comparatively good result in bad times, which enabled the Company slowly to complete their schemes before the severe general trade depression of the late 1880s had its effect.

In 1874 the enlargement of the Strand Station was complete, and a new running shed was built by Gradwell in 1874-5. The building of the Barrow Loop Line proceeded very slowly, Abbey Road Bridge being completed in 1875.

The Directors were determined to press on with the scheme to put Barrow on a through rail route and to connect the mines at Park with the Ironworks more directly. In 1875 a Bill was deposited for a line from the Hawcoat Branch at Cocken to join the main line at a point 29 chains north of the crossing at Thwaite Flat. Another line, leaving the Park Loop proper near Henry Schneider's mansion, Oak Lea, was to be built round to the Millwood Curve, reaching the latter north of the existing Park (Goldmire) Junction. These two lines were to be connected by a short curve of 2 furlongs, the old main line between Thwaite Flat and Millwood Junction being abandoned or used as a siding. The Bill also proposed an increase in capital of £750,000, in order to fund this project and the completion of Ramsden Dock. Finally, it contained powers to build a line from Plumpton Junction to Bardsea. It received Royal Assent on 29th June 1876.

Work on Ramsden Dock commenced in 1872 with the building of the outer sea dam from the mainland at Parrock Hall to the small island of Ramsey. This was followed by the embankment between Ramsey and Barrow Islands through which the entrance lock would be built, at the Ramsey Island end. The work was completed in 1874, and, as a result, a large area of sand was enclosed which would eventually form the Ramsden and Cavendish Docks. Work proceeded only very slowly after the enclosure, and, by 1876, the Board were becoming anxious about the amount of money being spent on the project. Consequently, before further contracts were placed, they asked for an estimate to be prepared of the cost likely to be incurred in completing the Docks. This showed that Ramsden Dock would need £150,000 and the embankment to separate the area designated for Cavendish

Ramsden Dock Basin, c.1899. *The impressivly uniformed officer is probably the FR Dock Master, Captain Wards, and his family. The four-masted barque is likely to be unloading iron ore.*
(From Sea Ports of the Furness Railway, Geoff Holme collection)

Top
Harbour Offices in
Ramsden Dock road.
(W Anderson collection
WH 17.4.2)

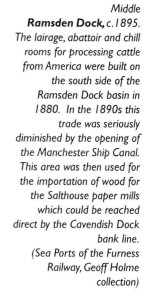

Middle
Ramsden Dock, c.1895.
The lairage, abattoir and chill
rooms for processing cattle
from America were built on
the south side of the
Ramsden Dock basin in
1880. In the 1890s this
trade was seriously
diminished by the opening of
the Manchester Ship Canal.
This area was then used for
the importation of wood for
the Salthouse paper mills
which could be reached
direct by the Cavendish Dock
bank line.
(Sea Ports of the Furness
Railway, Geoff Holme
collection)

Bottom
**Ramsden Dock Basin
North Side,** c.1930.
At top left can be seen the
sheds at the Anchor Line basin.
(Authors collection)

Dock would require a further £20,000. The Board must have been satisfied, as the works were sanctioned to continue.

Not all of the reclaimed land was to be used for the two new docks, for, in addition to the embankment enclosing the docks, a second embankment was to run north-west from the sea wall to join the Salthouse embankment just west of Salthouse Junction. Road access was provided by a new wider bridge over the Abbey Beck and a bridge under the main line, this new road, still in use, being west of the original crossing, passing the Sandgate Hotel on its west side before crossing the old main line.

Work on the entrance lock was held up because of the subsidence of one of the foundations, but the stonework was complete by the end of 1876 and the task of digging

out Ramsden Dock was commenced. The connection between the new dock and the existing Buccleuch Dock was by a cut in the Salthouse Embankment, although water was not allowed through until the horizontal swing bridge carrying the track of the Ramsden Dock Branch had been completed in 1879. Tide was admitted to the new dock on 12th June 1878 and, on 23rd March 1879, in the depths of the depression, the Ramsden Dock was formally opened. Cattle sheds were built on the south side of the entrance lock for the Merchant Trading Company, and an adjacent basin, used by the Anchor Line Steamships from the opening of the dock, is known to this day as the 'Anchor Line Basin'.

A line had been built from the old Channel Pier branch to the new entrance lock while this was under construction.

Barrow Shed, *September 1935, with ex-Furness No.20, now re-numbered by the LMSR as 12501. She was to survive into BR days as 52501 and was withdrawn in June 1957.* (Ken Norman, W Potter collection 412)

Barrow Shed. *No. 128 was built in 1901 by Sharp Stewart and became LMS 10145. She was scrapped in 1930.*
(George Taylor collection T94)

59

Shipyard Junction, *c.1900, looking east towards the original Buccleuch Dock Bridge. The branch to the left is to timber yards and to the right to the Ramsden Dock oil storage facilities. The two steamers laid up in the dock are Isle of Man Steam Packet Company vessels, the further one from the camera being* Empress Queen. *(George Taylor collection)*

At the end of the line the building of a passenger station, to serve the steamer traffic, was begun in 1880 to the north of the dock gates. Ramsden Dock Station in its final form had one bay platform, one through platform and two quayside roads, the latter for loading goods into ships moored at the deep water berth known as the Belfast Berth, dredged in the channel in 1884-5. The passenger platforms were covered by an all-over roof, and, on the opening of this Belfast Berth, the quayside was connected with the passenger platforms by two subways. The line continued through the station and curved round to join the north side sidings, reached by a goods line which left the main branch just before the new Ramsden Dock Road Bridge at a junction named Dockyard Junction. The south side sidings were reached by travelling to Salthouse Junction, then onto the Piel Branch as far as Parrock Hall, where a line branched off to the right and ran along the new embankment to Ramsey Island. A few years later a more direct route was provided by the building of a single line from the Swing Bridge to the south side which ran along the embankment separating the Ramsden and Cavendish Docks.

Ramsden Dock Station, *c.1885, viewed from Walney. The station was extended in 1885 so that two berths could be provided. The Barrow Steam Navigation company's* Donegal *lies at the Belfast Berth. At the new berth is a Furness Railway/James Little vessel, probably* Ariadne *used on the Barrow and Glasgow service. On the far right can be seen a Furness Railway 0-4-0 locomotive, probably either No. 3 or No. 4. The signal box dating from 1885 is visible on the extreme left, and was similar to the box still standing at Park South. (National Maritime Museum)*

Ramsden Dock Station. *The extended station of 1885 has* PS Duchess of Buccleuch *of the Barrow-Belfast service at her moorings.*
(Geoff Holme collection)

This connection faced towards the Channel so that goods traffic to and from the main line at Buccleuch Junction had to reverse. Road approach to the south side was by means of Cavendish Dock Road, a new road built in 1881, which ran from St George's Square, crossed over the old main line by a level crossing and passed under the new main line. The Ramsden Dock branch was avoided by a second under-line bridge, and the road then followed the embankment round to the south side. No attempt was made to dig out the Cavendish Dock, and from the outset it was used, as it is today, as a reservoir. It did however enjoy brief fame when leased to Vickers. Naval Airship No.1, more famously known as *Mayfly*, was built and berthed there, only to break its back while being pulled out of the shed in preparation for its maiden flight. The dock was also used for cooling water from Roosecote Power Station which, opened on 2nd June 1955, closed in 1986. The new gas-powered station on the site, opened on the 7th October 1991 by the then Secretary of State for Energy, John Wakeham, still uses the dock for this purpose.

Ramsden Dock Station, *c.1936, showing the interior of the passenger shed shortly before demolition.*   *(George Taylor collection)*

High Level bridge from Buccleuch Dock, c. 1900. Completed in 1886, together with new road approaches from Barrow town centre and Barrow Island, it created the present Michaelson Road. Prior to this a low level bridge crossed the passageway between the two docks. The bridge is seen open with a vessel entering Buccleuch Dock. (Geoff Holme collection)

While the Ramsden Dock work was being carried out great efforts were made to improve the rest of the Harbour. Early in 1874, a large dredger costing £22,000 was ordered from Barrow Shipbuilding Company, so that Piel Channel could be deepened to 9 feet at low water, spring tide, and widened to 100 feet, work commencing in 1877. In 1878, it was decided to widen the passageway between the Devonshire and Buccleuch Docks from 40 feet to 80 feet, and the contract was let to Gradwell for £11,150. At the same time, the building of a high level bridge over the Strand, Railway, Town Wharf and Passageway was planned but not commenced until 1881, when the work was let to Messrs Nelson and Company for £16,572, the first carriageway of

the bridge being opened in May 1882. The bridge was widened, with a second lifting and rolling portion being provided, in 1886. This bridge served ever-increasing traffic loads until the mid-1960s when complete reconstruction was needed, the work being completed in 1968.

From the opening of the Ramsden Dock, the old line from the Ramsden Dock Branch to the Channel Pier was used to give access to the Harbour Yard, a stretch of shore between the Pier and the Barrow Shipbuilding Company's Slipways, where the Barrow Steam Navigation Company's vessels were repaired. The Pier known as 'Glasgow Pier' from its use by James Little and Company's Barrow-Glasgow cargo service, in which the Furness Railway had an interest, was built in 1883.

High Level Bridge, c. 1966. The 1882-6 bridge was found to be subject to subsidence and in 1964 BR planned a replacement. This picture shows the first phase of the work in progress. One roadway was decommissioned and demolished while traffic still used the old west-bound carriageway. When the new east-bound carriageway was completed on 15th July 1967 this was opened, allowing the west-bound carriageway to be demolished and re-built, the official opening of the completed bridge taking place on 29th July 1968. In the right foreground is the long since closed Michaelson Bridge signal box. (Author MAA 20)

During these years of depression the Barrow Loop proceeded very slowly. Work was restricted to earthworks in 1876, and in June 1877 Gradwell's tender of £8,850 for the proposed Salthouse Viaduct was accepted. As originally intended, the Barrow Loop commenced at Salthouse Junction, the junction for the Stank and Piel lines, and curved round sharply to the north-west, crossing the old Timber Pond and original main line embankment. From this point a curve was built round to Buccleuch Junction which, besides enabling through running from the Barrow Loop to Barrow Yard and Ramsden Dock, gave a new means of access to the engine shed and railway works. The engine shed sidings joined this curve at Loco Junction, where a signal box was built. Access was also provided for Claye's Works by a line parallel to the main line of the Barrow Loop from Salthouse Junction, and which descended steeply to pass under the curve by means of two under-line bridges. These two bridges, after years of disuse, were only filled in during the 1950s, and the abutments of the more northerly one could still be seen long after that. The junction, just south of the present Salthouse Road bridge, was called 'St Luke's Junction' after the nearby church. On 17th August 1890, a new Loco Junction signal box was opened, which combined the functions of the former Buccleuch and Loco Junction boxes.

From St Luke's Junction, the line crossed Salthouse Road by means of the Salthouse Viaduct. This had eight brick arches, and a metal road span which was replaced by the present span in 1977. It then passed in a straight line to Cocken. The first part of the line followed the course of an existing narrow gauge tramway built about 1873 by William Gradwell. He was then engaged in the rapid construction of dwelling houses and shops in Barrow and Hindpool, and had established his own brick works on the east side of the Dalton Road where there was plenty of good clay. The clay was brought to his works, Dalton Road Brickworks, by means of two tramways, one running to a clay pit near the Rolling Mill at Ainslie Street and the other in the opposite direction, towards Salthouse. The Barrow Loop Line, being built from Salthouse to the Rolling Mill siding, thus followed the course of these tramways. On the laying of the track of the Loop Line the tramway was on its eastern side, and reached the brickworks on the western side by means of a tunnel. These tramways remained until 1895 when the brickworks was converted into a sawmill by Gradwell's nephews William and John Dawson. The tramway remains were obliterated by the building of Platform 4 of Barrow Central Station, which opened on 5th May 1907. From Abbey Road Bridge, the line passed through the site of the intended new station and on to Devonshire Road Bridge, where it was joined by the Rolling Mill Siding.

By 1878 the Barrow Loop earthworks were not yet complete, so a Bill was deposited to renew the powers and to extend the Loop to join the Park Loop to be built from the Hawcoat Branch. The Bill also applied for permission to work a Ferry between Walney Island and Barrow Island, and to build the 'Furness and Midland Curve' into Carnforth main station. By 1880 the Park Loop powers had also lapsed, so another Bill was deposited for the renewal of these powers and, in February 1881, the Park Loop Contract was

Salthouse Road Bridge, 1956, situated at the southern end of the Barrow Loop Line opened in 1882. 2-6-4 tank No. 42359 of Barrow shed (11B) heads an excursion to Morecambe. The signal shown behind the locomotive controlled the junction for trains travelling south along the main line or direct to the engine sheds and the docks. St Luke's Junction signalbox shown on page 5 is just to the left of the picture. This bridge was replaced during the late 1970s by the single span bridge still in use today.   (CRA Worden collection WOR271)

Salthouse Junction, c.1959. 4F 0-6-0 No. 44469 heads east with a Barrow - Carnforth freight. (Author MAA 11)

let to Messrs Ward and Company for £18,987, the work commencing immediately. The new Park Loop Act of 1881 did not include the scheme to replace the original main line between Thwaite Flat and Millwood, as this was now considered an unnecessary expense. The loop was authorised to join the main line at a point south of Thwaite Flat Crossing by means of the present 11 chains curve with its 10 m.p.h. speed restriction, eased to 20 m.p.h. in recent years.

The Barrow Loop was nearing completion by August 1881, and the Park Loop was progressing. On 1st June 1881 the first train ran into Ramsden Dock Station. To avoid confusion, Barrow's existing station in the Strand was

renamed 'Barrow Town'. The Isle of Man Boat Trains used the new station during the summer and the Belfast Mail Boats continued to run to Piel. However, at the close of the season on 1st October these ran to Ramsden Dock in place of the Isle of Man trains, the last train running from Furness Abbey to Piel direct on 30th September. The service on the Piel Line was maintained by trains running direct from Barrow to Piel, and on 27th March 1882 the line between Roose Junction and Parrock Hall was closed. The site of this line could be plainly seen until the extension of the gasworks was built in 1952, when the bridge under the Stank Line was filled in and the formation beyond covered by a

Salthouse Junction, 1st April 1967. An unidentified Britannia hauls a short van train. On the right one of Barrow's diesel shunters waits with a train of empty coal hoppers from Roosecote Power Station. This line was the former Piel Loop of 1873. In the centre distance is the stub of the Stank Branch. (Author MAA 9)

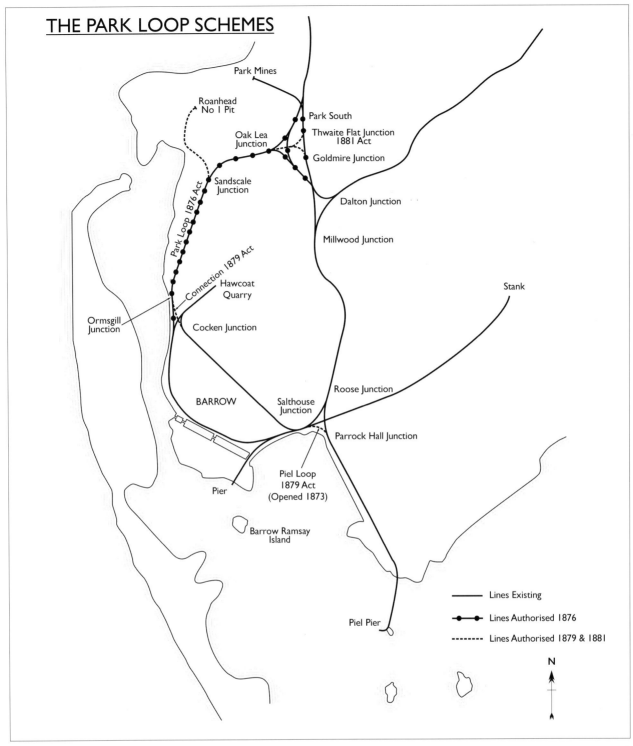

THE PARK LOOP SCHEMES

Park Mines

Roanhead
No I Pit

Oak Lea
Junction

Park South

Thwaite Flat Junction
1881 Act

Goldmire Junction

Dalton Junction

Sandscale
Junction

Millwood Junction

Park Loop 1876 Act

Stank

Connection 1879 Act

Hawcoat
Quarry

Ormsgill
Junction

Cocken Junction

BARROW

Salthouse
Junction

Roose Junction

Parrock Hall Junction

Pier

Piel Loop
1879 Act
(Opened 1873)

Barrow Ramsay
Island

Piel Pier

———	Lines Existing
—•—•—	Lines Authorised 1876
- - - - -	Lines Authorised 1879 & 1881

N

concrete floor for tipping coal. Parrock Hall remained as a ground-frame which controlled the siding into the nearby sand-pits until the Piel Branch was closed from this point onwards on 6th July 1936. In 1954 the branch was re-built as far as the new Roosecote Power Station which received all its coal by rail, trains running into a re-modelled yard adjacent to the Docks lines at Salthouse, reversing over the junction onto the old Piel line, past the Gasworks and into the Power Station. This too has now closed and the present gas-powered station is on the site.

By 1st June of 1882 the Park and Barrow Loops were complete, the new timetable was brought into operation and the new Central Station opened. This had three roads, the most westerly serving No. I Down Main Platform where the

main buildings of the station had been constructed in wood. The other two tracks ran on each side of the island platform, No. 2 being the Up Main and No. 3 a reversible road.

Platforms I and 2 were covered by an all-over roof but not No. 3, on the east side of which was the tramway to the clay pits. There were signal boxes at each end of the island platform, and the carriage sidings were at the north end of the station. Adjacent to the north end of No. I platform were two short bays for the unloading of mail and perishable goods, still known as the Fish Dock, from where a long siding curved back to the Abbey Road, later called the 'Duke' siding after the nearby Duke of Edinburgh Hotel. There was a loop alongside the Down line, from St. Luke's Junction to Barrow South which, as well as providing

THE FURNESS RAILWAY.

For several Trains not given in the Columns, see the statements at the bottom of the Columns.

UP					WEEK DAYS.														SUNDAYS			
	1	2	3	4	5	6	7	8	9	10	11	12	13	14	15	16	17	18	19	1	2	3-4	5
Carlisle ..de						a m				a m 6 40	a m 9 10					a m 1045		p m 3 30	p m 5 35		a m		a m 8 30
Cockerm'th										8 50	1034					1D45		2 44					8 28
Workington						6 0				9 15	1059					2 16		5 57	7 0		8 15		10 0
Whiteha'n a						6 20				9 35	1115					2 35		5 2	7 20		8 28		1020
Whiteha'n				a*m	a m	a m	a m	a m	a m	9 50	1120	* *	p*m	p m		p*m 2 40	p m	5 40	7 30	a m	7 10		8 33 5 45
Corkickle						6 55				9 54	1124					2 44		5 44	7 34		7 14		8 37 5 49
St. Bees ..						6 59				10 3	1133					2 53		5 53	7 43		7 23		8 40 5 58
Nethertov'n						7 3				10 9						2 39		6 4			7 29		6 4
Braystones						7 14				1014						3 4		6 9			7 34		6 9
						7 19																	
Moor Rowde						6 53					1119							5 43					
Egremont ..						7 2					1127							5 52					
Sellafield ar						7 15					114							6 5					
Sellafield de						7 24				1019	1145		Saturdays Only.			3 9		6 14	7 55		7 39		6 14
Seascale...						7 29				1024	1150					3 14		6 19	8 0		7 44	9 0	6 19
Drigg						7 34				1029	I					3 19		6 24			7 49		6 24
Ravenglass						7 39				1034	1153					3 24		6 29			7 54	9 7	6 29
Eskmeals ..						7 3				1038						3 28		6 33			7 58		6 33
Bootle.....						7 50				1045	I					3 35		6 40			8 5		6 40
Silecroft..						8 1				1056						3 46		6 51			8 25		6 51
Millom						8 10	9 30			11 5	1221			2 10		3 56	5 0	7 0	8 26		8 25	9 29	7 0
Green Road						8 16	9 36			1111				2 16			5 6	7			8 31		7 6
Foxfield ar						8 20	9 40			1115	1228			2 20		4 3	5 10	7 10			8 35		7 10
Foxfield..de						8 23				1123	3 8	3 8				5 18		5 22			8 53		7 18
Broughton..						8 27				1127	3 12	3 12				5 22		5 29			8 57		7 22
Woodland ..						8 34				1134	3 19	3 19				5 29		5 38			9 4		7 29
Torver						8 43				1143	3 28	3 28				5 38		5 45			9 13		7 38
Conist'n La'e						8 50				1150	3 35	3 35				5 45					9 20		7 45
Coniston L'ed					7 20			9 10	1045							2 35	4 40				8 5		6 40
Torver					7 26			9 16	1051							2 41	4 46				8 11		6 46
Woodland ..					7 35			9 25	11 0							2 50	4 55				8 20		6 55
Broughton					7 43	8 13		9 33	11 8							2 58	5 3				8 28		7 3
Foxfie'd ..ar					7 47	8 17		9 37	1112							3 2	5 7				8 32		7 7
Foxfield de						8 22	9 42			1117	1230		2 22		4 5	5 12					8 37		7 12
Kirkby ..						8 28	9 48			1123			2 28			5 18	7 12	7 12			8 43		7 18
Askam						8 36	9 56			1131	1241		2 36			5 26	7 18				8 51		7 26
Barrow C.S a						8 50				1145	1255		2 50		4 25	5 40	7 26	8 41		9 5	9 55	7 40
d																	7 40	8 55				
Ram Dockar																	7 48				Stop	
																	7 55					
	a*m	a m	a*m	a m * *		a m	a*m			a m	a m p*m	* *	p*m		p m * *	p m	p m	p m * *		a m	a n	p m	p m
Ram. Dock d			7 8															6 50					
Barrow C.S.a																							
d	6 25	7 0		7 50		8 55				1150	1240	1 0	1 55		2 55	4 10	4 30		9 0	7 0	9 10	4 45	7 45
Roose.....		7 5	G			9 0				1155			3 0			5 50		7 45		7 5	9 15	4 50	7 50
Furness Ab	7 10	G	H		9 5				12 0	1248		2 3			5 55		7 50		7 10	9 20	4 55	7 55
Dalton		7 15				9 10	10 7			12 5	1253		2 8		3 10	6 0		7 55		7 15	9 25	5 0	8 0
Lindal		7 20		8 6		9 15	1012			1210				3 15	6 8		9 7		7 20	9 30	5 8	8 5
Ulverston ar	6 44	7 27	7 30	8 6		9 22	1020			1218	1 4	1 16	2 19		3 23	4 34	4 46		8 13	9 19	7 28	9 38 5 13	8 13
Ulverston de						9 23	1025				1 10				3 30		5 10	7 0	7 9		9 40	5 20	
Greenodd ..						9 32	1034				1 19				3 39		5 19	7 16			9 49	5 29	
Haverthw'te						9 39	1041				1 26				3 46		5 26	7 25			9 56	5 36	
Lake Side ar						9 47	1050				1 35				3 55		5 35				10 55	5 45	
Lake Side de						9 55					1 40				4 10								
Bowness						1080					2 15				4 45								
Ambleside ar						11 5					2 50				5 20								
Ambleside de									8 40	1120			2 55										
Bowness									9 10	1150			3 25										
Lake Side ar									9 50	1230			4 5										
Lake Side de						8 25			9 53	1235		2 25	4 10				6 25				4 45	5 50	
Haverthw'te						8 43				1	1243		2 33	4 18				6 33				4 53	5 58	
Greenodd ..						8 50			10 8	1250		2 40	4 25				6 40				5 0	6 5	
Ulverston ar						9 0			1017	1 0		2 50	4 35				6 50				5 10	6 15	
Ulverston de		7 31		8 7		9 26				1221	1 7	1 18	2 22		3 26	4 37	4 48	6 16	8 16	9 21	7 31	5 16	8 16
Dark & Car'l		7 44				9 39				1234					3 39			6 29	8 29		7 44	5 29	8 29
Kent Bank		7 50				9 45				1240					3 45			6 35	8 35		7 50	5 35	8 35
Grange ..ar		7 54		8 22		9 49				1244	1 22		2 37		3 49	4 52		6 39	8 39		7 54	5 39	8 39
Grange ..de		7 56		8 25		9 51				1246	1 24		2 39		3 51	4 54		6 41	8 41		7 56	5 41	8 41
Arnside ..		8 5		8 33		10 0				1255					4 0	I		6 50	8 50		8 5	5 50	8 50
Silverdale ..		8 11				10 6				1 0					4 6			6 56	8 56		8 11	5 56	8 56
Carnforth ar		8 20		8 45		1015				1 10	1 40	1 47	2 55		4 15	5 10	5 17	7 9	9 9	9 50	8 20	6 9	9 5
Carnforth de		9 25		9 25		1113				1 21	1 58	3 50		4 26		5 58	8 7		1021		6 10		
Kendal ..ar		1015		1015		1150				1 54	2 40	4 20		4 52		6 25	8 41		1045		6 50		
Carlisle ...		1145		1145		1 5				3 5	4 10	5 40									8 18		
Carnforth de		8 30				1035				1 55	3 0				6 5			12 0	8 25		6 15		12 0
Wennington		8 46				1054				2 10	3 20				6 29				8 45		6 40		
Skipton ...		9 35				12 0				3 0	4 20				7 46			1011		7 55		10 0	
Bradford ..		1020				1 0				3 50	5 15				8 38			1 45	1112		8 55	1 45	
Leeds		1020				1 5				3 45	5 10				8 45			1 49	1138		9 33	1 49	
Sheffield...		1135				2 20				4 52	6 35				1124			3 50	4 3		1116	3 50	
Derby		1235				3 40				6 57	9 15				1230			5 35	5 55		1220	5 35	
London, S P		3 20				6 5				8 40	1020				4 15			8 20	9 55		4 15	8 20	
Carnforth de		8 22		8 50		1029				1 52	3 18		4 23		5 23	7 12		9 55	9 50		6 52	10 6	
Morecambe a		9 20		9 20		11 2					6 57	40		4 55		5 57							
Lancaster ..		8 36		9 0		1038				2 1	3 27		4 40		5 32	7 21		10 4	1010		7 13		
Preston ..a		9 32		9 32		1110				2 30	4 0		5 45		6 57	55			1035		8 15	1042	
Man. V... a		1040		1040		1227					3 t85	10	—	7 20		7 33	9 0		1210		10 0		
Liverpool Ex		1028		1028		1225					4 27	5 30				7 28	52				1010		
Man. Ex. ..		1030		1030		1241						6 12				7 12	8 58						
Liv. Lime St		1048		1048		1240					3 50	5 40				7 50	9 10		12 0			12 0	
Crewe		1135		1135		1230					3 40	6 0				7 33			12 8			12 7	
Birmingham						2 45					5 55	7 55				9 15			2 32			2 32	
London, Eu.		3 30		3 30		4 15					7 0	1015					1050		3 50			3 50	

☞ ON SATURDAYS ONLY a train leaves Barrow C.S. at 10-45 p.m.: Dalton, 10-55 ; Lindal, 11-0 ; arriving at Ulverston, 11-8.

Furness Railway Time Table, *from Soulby's Ulverston Advertiser, 3rd November 1892.* (Geoff Holme collection)

Hawcoat Branch south sidings, c.1948, from Devonshire Road bridge. On the left is the double line into the Ward's plant, a site formerly occupied by the Griffin furnace, and the single line to Dawson's Central Sawmills. These sidings were controlled by Hawcoat Branch ground frame. On the right are the Central Station carriage sheds. (Peter Holmes)

an extra through running road, gave access to several works on the down side of the line between the north end of Salthouse Viaduct and Central Station.

From the Central Station the line continued to the Hawcoat Branch. It had been intended to cross the branch on the level but, with the completion of the dock work, it had become less important. Instead, the line was connected to the Barrow Loop only, by means of a trailing junction with the Up goods road which served the New Iron Works (as the Rolling Mill was now called). As noted, the Hawcoat Branch had, however, been moved onto a new embankment during the 1870s, as it had been found that the original

embankment was too low to permit the bridging of the new Schneider Road. So a second bank was built on the south-east side of the old one, and the altitude gained was not wasted as the line was then continued to a new, higher part of the quarry. The Hindpool end of the Hawcoat Branch was continued along the west side of the Barrow Loop and reception sidings were built, this extension of the branch (officially the first part of the Park Loop) joining the main line at Ormsgill Junction. The Hawcoat Branch trailing junction was controlled by a second signal box, Cocken Junction, in the sidings on the Down side; this box did not control the main line.

Dawson's siding, 1947. Ex-LNWR coal engine No. 28128 of Barrow shed (11B) has delivered a load of logs and poses with the sawmill staff. In the background is Ward's rotary furnace known as the 'White Elephant' (the author is second from the left). (Author's collection)

Barrow Central, *c.1907. On the left is 0-4-0 No. 3 in its glass case, preserved after a working life of 55 years. (Geoff Holme collection)*

From Ormsgill Junction the line ran, rising slowly in a north-east direction with the sea on the down side and Sowerby Woods on the up side. The summit was near Sandscale, at which point the line turned sharply eastwards, and a level crossing was provided a few yards north of the present Automatic Crossing. On this curve was the junction with the single line Sandscale Branch, which curved away to the left to Pit No. 1 of Roanhead Mines. There was a signal box, Sandscale Junction, on the down side, which controlled both the Crossing and the Junction. By 1899 this box was only opened as required, and the branch and box were finally closed on 9th July 1933. The main line fell gradually from here to Oak Lea Junction where the lines to Park South and Goldmire for Dalton diverged.

It then curved sharply round to join the original line at Thwaite Flat Junction, where a new signal box was provided. The level crossing here was controlled by a second box, the present Park South, which also controlled the entrance to Park sidings and the junction for the private line to Park Mines. This was found to be an extravagant arrangement, so the control of the junction was taken over by Park South and Thwaite Flat Junction box was abolished on 15th September 1890.

The completion of these works enabled trains between Carnforth and Whitehaven to call at Barrow without reversal. Another great advantage was that iron ore from Park and coke from Durham could be run directly into the Ironworks via Oak Lea Junction and Ormsgill Junction.

Barrow Central, *c.1899, before the wooden buildings on platform 1 were replaced. Inside the trainshed, 4-4-0 No. 36 waits with a southbound stopping train in platform 2.*
(CRA Kerr collection KER051)

Barrow Central Platform 4, *April 1955. This platform was built in 1907. On the far left is the Barrow Central North signal box, opened in July 1907, which replaced an earlier structure opened when the station was built in 1882. At the end of platform 4 can be seen the former Piel signal box, re-located and used by the Signal Department. The platform 4 line was closed in 1970.* (Author MAC 84)

Barrow Central, *c.1936, a panoramic view from the top of the cooling tower of Barrow Electricity Works. In the foreground is the new Post Office, Barrow Central South signal box and Abbey Road bridge. Middle left is the Duke siding curving round towards Abbey Road. Behind the station are the extensive carriage sheds. In the distance, right, is Ward's rotary furnace and Dawson's Central Sawmills, both being served by sidings off the Hawcoat Branch.* (Derek Lyon collection)

***Oak Lea Junction site,** c.1935. An FR illuminated 10 mph speed limit sign is at the beginning of the sharp curve round to Park South on the main line from Barrow. The original more favourable alignments had to be abandoned in 1881 to reduce expenditure. In the background is Goldmire Quarry which supplied limestone to Millom Ironworks.*   *(CRA Pattinson collection PA97)*

Between 1870 and 1881 the timetable had changed in only one important respect. At the end of April 1873, the time-consuming reversal at Furness Abbey had been abandoned and trains ran direct to Whitehaven via the Millwood Curve. From this time Furness Abbey was included in the Barrow Branch, passengers to and from Barrow changing at Dalton. The only passenger train using the old main line between Millwood and Goldmire Junctions was an afternoon train from Coniston to Furness Abbey and back. The Down Belfast Boat Train passengers left St Pancras at 10.00 a.m. arriving at Piel at 7.10 p.m. in 1870. By 1880 this had been accelerated, leaving St Pancras at 12.15 p.m., arriving at Piel at 8.15 p.m., and the 10.00 a.m. had become the Isle of Man Boat Train. The down mail from Euston had been decelerated, now reaching Whitehaven at 7.15 a.m.

The timetable for June 1882 was completely altered. The sub-table for the 'Barrow Branch' disappeared and the main line included Furness Abbey, Roose and Barrow Central Stations. Ramsden Dock Station was given a separate line between 'Central arrival' and 'Central departure'. There were 16 down trains and 18 up trains on weekdays, the slow trains taking about 1 hour 20 minutes from Carnforth to Barrow and expresses less than 1 hour. There were three Isle of Man Boat Trains, the fastest the 10.00 a.m. from St Pancras (with a change at Leeds), stopping only at Furness Abbey. The train left Leeds at 2.40 p.m. and arrived at Ramsden Dock at 5.15 p.m. taking only 2 hours 35 minutes over this journey! The Piel Branch had three trains a day in each direction.

***Barrow Iron Works Slag Bank,** 1947. The site of Cocken Junction is in the centre of the picture. On the extreme left is the Hawcoat branch bridge over Walney Road. The line on the extreme right was used by Barrow Ironworks to propel slag ladles, illustrated on page 94, to the top of the slag bank for tipping.*   *(Author MAB 6)*

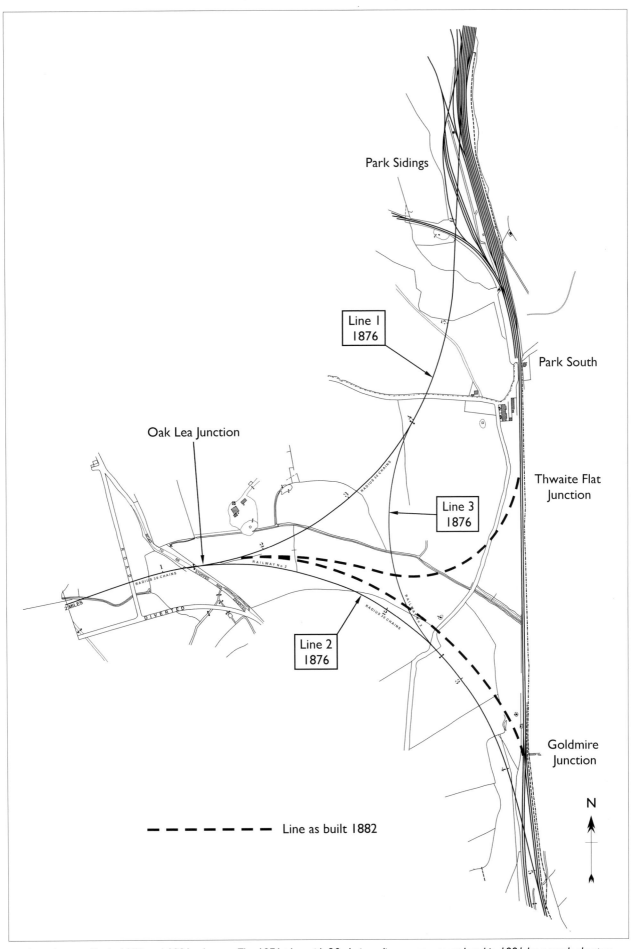

Park Sidings

Line 1
1876

Park South

Oak Lea Junction

Thwaite Flat
Junction

Line 3
1876

Line 2
1876

Goldmire
Junction

N

— — — — — — Line as built 1882

Junctions at Park, *1876 and 1881 schemes. The 1876 plan with 30 chain radius curves was replaced in 1881 by a much cheaper scheme but with an 11 chain curve carrying a speed restriction of 10 mph.*

Park South signal box,
c.1935. This signalbox, designed by architects Paley & Austin, dates from 16th June 1883 and is of the distnctive style used by the FR at this time. In 1890 Park South took over the function of nearby Thwaite Flat Junction.
(CRA Pattinson collection PA112)

Park South, c.1974, a view looking north showing the crossing gates and crossing cottage. The cottage, built in 1849 has now been demolished, and the wooden gates controlled by a big wheel in the signal box have now been replaced by modern lifting barriers.
(J Martin Hurst,
Ken Norman collection)

Park South, c.2003. Workmen's trains are still run from Sellafield to Barrow daily and here class 153 single car unit 153 310 pilots a two-car class 156 unit on this working. The tranquillity of the Goldmire Valley has been shattered by the building of the A590 Dalton bypass bridge immediately behind the box, the new route into Barrow opening on 17th December 1993.
(Alan Johnstone AJ-03-6209)

Chapter 14: The Final Years of the Ramsden Era

The early 1880s had been quite prosperous years. There had been no return to the 10% dividend, but there had been a sufficient increase in traffic after the depression of the 1870s to justify the completion of the great schemes. Ramsden Dock Station and the Barrow and Park Loops had been opened at the height of this prosperity, but as early as 1883 traffic yet again began to fall off, and by 1884 an even more severe and widespread trade depression had set in. Passenger traffic was not unduly diminished, so some minor projects were continued. The Bardsea Branch had been opened on 27th June 1883, and by August of that year the Piel Bar dredging had been completed to a depth of 9 feet at low water spring tide. The widening of the Channel was completed the next year and the dredging of the Belfast Berth begun, being finished in 1885. In this year the station was enlarged and a second steamer berth provided.

The fall-off in freight traffic was so considerable in 1883 that the Railway Works staff were put on short time, and, on 16th October, wages paid by the Company were cut by 5%, a reduction which continued until an improvement in trade began in 1887. As a result of this depression the dividend to Shareholders fell from 7.5% to 5% at the end of 1883 and still further to 2% at the end of 1886.

With the slight improvement of 1887 came three new commercial projects. The American Food Supply Syndicate approached the FR Company with a plan to use Barrow Docks as their point of import, but this unfortunately came to nothing. In April 1888, 20 acres of land, which had been reclaimed by the building of the Cavendish Dock Embankment, were sold to Mr Partington as a site for a paper mill. This Works, completed in 1890, was known as the Barrow Chemical Wood Pulp Company. The southern-most line of the double Piel Loop was, from this time, used as a siding to the works and as an approach to the single line on the Cavendish Dock Embankment, the Piel trains using the northern-most line only. The third project was the establishment in Barrow of the petroleum industry, large storage tanks, now used for gas condensate storage, being built on the north side of the Anchor Line Basin off Ramsden Dock. The Railway Company contributed to the cost of building these tanks, in return for a guaranteed yearly import. The tanks were completed in 1899.

Improvements were carried out at Ramsden Dock and Central Stations at this time, refreshment rooms being provided. The Midland Railway agreed to pay the cost of the Ramsden Dock improvements, but refused to cover

Ramsden Dock, *July 1920, an aerial view looking north east. In the foreground is the Basin with the former foreign cattle facility removed in the 1930s then being used for the importation of wood for Salthouse paper mills on the right. Beyond is the east end of the Anchor Line Basin. A narrow bridge carrying a single line of rail and a footpath encloses the timber pond and beyond is the extensive oil storage depot built in 1888 and disused from around 1929 apart from being retained as a strategic oil reserve during World War 2. The gas condensate plant for the new gas-powered Roosecote power station now occupies the site.* (Aerofilms 4066)

Ramsden Dock Basin north side, c.1917. Iron ore is being unloaded by use of grabs. This method, adopted during the 1914-18 war, greatly increased the rate of discharge of iron ore carriers which were handled at Barrow to supply West Cumberland and Lancashire furnaces. (CRA Walker collection)

the Furness Company's loss in running certain of the Boat Expresses. As a reprisal, the Furness cut the Boat Train Service by one train.

During these difficult years the Furness Company proprietors' subsidiary interests had fared much worse than the railway itself. The Barrow Shipbuilding Company, having nearly collapsed in 1878, did so in 1888 and was re-floated as the Naval Construction and Armaments Company. On 25th May 1879 and again on 8th June 1892 the Barrow Flax and Jute Company's works were partially destroyed by fire. After many years of struggle it was sold in 1897, and finally closed down shortly after the conclusion of the First World War.

The Regulation of Railways Act of 1889 had severe repercussions on the Furness Company. In 1890 the following requirements were laid down by the Board of Trade:-

1. The Block System must be adopted within 12 months on passenger lines.
2. All points and signals must be interlocked.
3. All passenger coaches must be fitted with continuous brake within 2 years.

This work was not finally completed until 1898.

From the opening of the Loop lines in 1882 until 1895 there were few notable timetable changes. After the exchange of many letters, the FR agreed to the Dalton Local

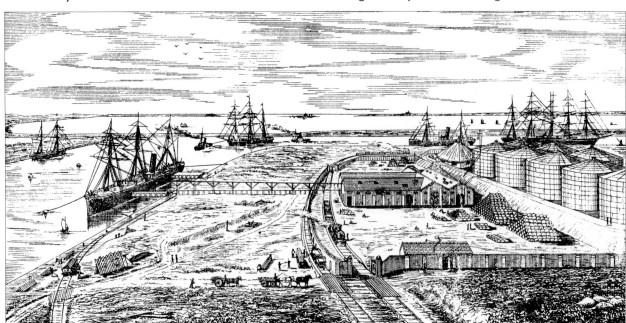

Ramsden Dock, c.1892, a print of the oil storage facility. In the foreground is the line to Shipyard Junction. Petroleum importation began in 1888. (Geoff Holme collection)

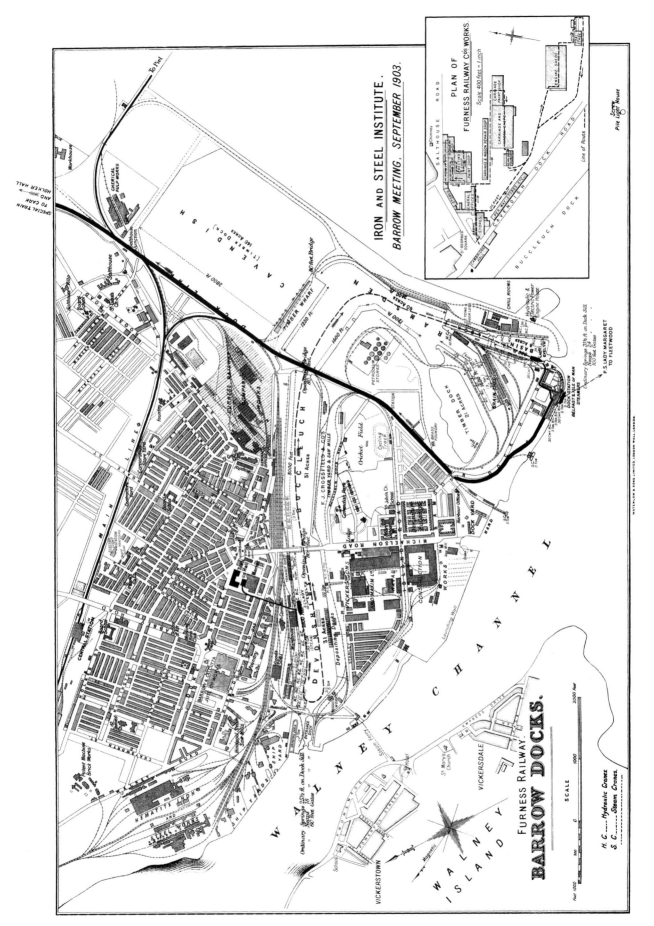

Barrow Docks Plan, *from a Furness Railway presentation book for the Iron and Steel Institute Barrow Meeting, September 1903.*

(Geoff Holme collection)

Top
Walney Channel, *27th July 1895.* HMS Powerful *is launched from the slipway of Barrow Shipyard.*

Middle
Devonshire Dock, *c.1896, showing the FR Transit Shed (right) and bonded warehouse (left). FR owned steam tender Scout is being used for torpedo trials.*

Bottom
Barrow Shipyard, *c.1896, an artists impression of a panoramic view of the shipyard.*

(All Vickers, Sons and Maxim 'The Works', Geoff Holme collection)

Board's demand for direct trains to run between Dalton and Askam, and in 1885 the 'Local Board Train' ran from Millom to Ulverston and back each day via the Millwood Curve. The last passenger train to use the line between Millwood and Goldmire, that running from Coniston to Furness Abbey and back, ceased at the end of September 1890.

The early 1890s saw trade yet again falling off. A severe national crisis was caused by the Durham Miners' strike of 1892, which locally closed the iron and steel works. From this time on things became worse, causing the Barrow Haematite Steel Company, the last of the Furness Railway proprietors' outside interests, to struggle for survival. Once considered inexhaustible, the iron ore mines of Furness had started to be less productive in the 1880s, and by the 1890s the older ones were becoming worked out.

Even more serious had been the introduction of a new steel-making process which could use cheaper ironstone from Cleveland and the South Midlands, and thus the high quality, expensive haematite steel, which used mainly haematite ore, became less competitive. By the 1890s the Bessemer Plant, once the largest and most up to date in the British Isles, was obsolescent, and the BHS Company had to cut its steel prices to keep in the market. The Furness Railway Company reduced its carrying charges to the Steel Works in an attempt to keep the latter working, but in 1895, in the depths of the depression and after many reductions in charges, the works was closed for some months. The dividend on FR Ordinary Stock fell to zero for the first half of 1895.

The iron ore mining, which had been carried out so extensively for so many years, began, in the 1890s, to affect the railway line in the mining districts. An engine had been lost at Lindal on 22nd September 1892, and a further small subsidence occurred the following year on

the edge of the same site. In 1894, after a protracted argument with Messrs Harrison and Ainslie of Lindal Moor Mines, a survey was carried out with a view to building a new main line from the Bardsea Branch to Salthouse should the main line become impassable because of subsidence. Harrison and Ainslie were eventually persuaded not to carry out any more mining under the main line, and this diversion was never necessary.

The year 1894 saw the end of Piel Pier. Although the cause of much trouble in the early days of the Furness Railway, it had not become important until the commencement of the Midland Boat Trains in 1867. Its active years had been few as, with the opening of Ramsden Dock Station in 1881, it fell out of use, but survived until 1894 when it was finally dismantled. Before this, a new station had been built on Roa Island for the local traffic. This had one platform, an overall roof, and was situated on the west side of the Roa Island Hotel. The few sidings were controlled by a signal box on the Barrow end of the platform. There were 6 trains a day in each direction during the 1890s.

1895 can be looked upon as the end of a great industrial era in Furness. Seeing his great industrial empire crumbling and his docks half derelict, Sir James Ramsden retired in this year. He died at his home, Abbot's Wood, on the hill overlooking Furness Abbey, just over a year later on 19th October 1896. His last appearance in public had been on 24th July 1895, at the launch of *HMS Powerful* from the shipyard on Barrow Island. His enterprise and ambition had turned a rural corner of England into a roaring, smoky industrial centre, but the geographical remoteness and exhaustion of the iron ore had prevented the realisation of Ramsden's vision of *a Liverpool, Sheffield and Birmingham all rolled into one.*

Piel Station on Roa Island, *c.1910. In the centre is the Roa Island Hotel, built as the Piel Pier Hotel. When the Midland Railway Belfast and Isle of Man steamers were transferred from Morecambe to Piel Pier in 1867, the FR developed Roa Island, building houses for their staff. On the right is the Roa Island gasworks. An unidentified 2-4-0 has just arrived with a train from Barrow Central. (Lawrence Allen collection)*

Top
Abbot's Wood Entrance Court, *c. 1896.*
This mansion above Furness Abbey was built by the Furness Railway Company for their Secretary & Manager James Ramsden. Commenced in 1857 it was added to over the years. Ramsden became the FR Managing Director, founded the Borough of Barrow and was knighted in 1872; his son Frederick, also a FR and later LMSR director lived at Abbot's Wood until his death in 1941. After wartime use the mansion was demolished.
Middle
Abbot's Wood Dining Room.
Bottom
Steam Yacht Aries II *owned by Sir James was built at Barrow and launched 25th November 1881.*
(All Cumbria Record Office & Local History Library, Barrow LC291 VB/ABB)

The resignation of Sir James Ramsden from his post as Managing Director of the Furness Railway in May 1895 could not have come at a worse time for the appointment of a successor. The Barrow Haematite Steel Company, one of the FR's main customers, had reported that *a large reduction in rates is necessary to enable the company to continue the manufacture of steel.* In spite of such reductions being given, the steelworks closed down for three months later in the year. A further problem was that the FR directors had found themselves unable to pay any dividend on the Ordinary Shares of the FR for the first time since the national financial crisis of 1848! But the FR had strengths. The Chairman was that veteran of both Commons front benches, Spencer Cavendish, former Marquis of Hartington and, since 1891, 8th Duke of Devonshire. He was supported by Henry Cook, the Secretary and Traffic Manager, a railway manager of great experience and proven ability. They decided to seek the advice of a company uninvolved in FR matters, the Caledonian Railway. Charles Scotter and James Thompson of the 'Caley' recommended that the post should be designated 'General Manager', reporting to the Board. On the subject of a candidate, they recommended Alfred Aslett, General Manager of the Cambrian Railways. Aslett (1847-1928) had started his railway career on the Great Northern Railway in 1862.

In 1884 he became Manager of the Eastern & Midlands Railway (later the Midland & Great Northern Joint), and in 1891 was made General Manager of the Cambrian Railways where, according to the Railway Magazine of July 1913, he developed the traffic *to a remarkable extent.* He was offered a salary of £1,500 per annum rising to £1,800 after three years. Aslett accepted, and took up his new post in October 1895. The high level of this salary can be judged by the fact that William Pettigrew, a locomotive engineer of note, was recruited to the FR as Locomotive, Carriage and Wagon Superintendent at an initial salary of £600 per annum.

Aslett, as well as his experience, had good fortune on his side, as his arrival at Barrow coincided with an upturn in the activity of the iron trade. He was able to concentrate on the things he did best, the development of passenger traffic and the reduction of operating expenses. In respect of passenger traffic, the Regulation of Railways Act 1889 had, among its several requirements, the application of continuous brakes to passenger trains. Ramsden, some years before, had warned the FR Board that the old four-wheeled passenger coaches would not withstand the stresses resulting from continuous brakes, and a programme of building six-wheeled stock was already under way. Tourist bookings had been introduced as early as 1859 when the *Gondola* first sailed on Coniston Water.

Barrow Graving Dock, *c.1904. Inside the dock, opened in August 1882, a ship is being lengthened. This is thought to be the FR* Lady Evelyn *used on the Furness Railway Barrow to Fleetwood service and which was lengthened in 1904.* (Authors collection)

Barrow Central, *c.1900. The traffic staff pose for an official photograph. On the extreme left is Arthur Atkinson who in later years became Station Inspector.*
(Ken Norman collection)

When the FR reached Windermere at Lakeside in 1869, the possibility of 'Circular Tours' of the Lakes was recognised by Henry Cook. These possibilities were further increased when the Arnside to Hincaster Junction line opened in 1876 giving access to the LNWR station at Windermere Town. The gaps between the railway and steamer stations were covered by horse drawn omnibuses running between Ambleside and Coniston, Coniston Lake Bank and Greenodd, and between Windermere Town and Bowness. Henry Cook's four tours were quickly increased to twenty by Aslett. These, subject to minor variations, continued until curtailed by the 1914-18 war, but were resumed after the war and continued to a limited extent into LMS days.

One of these tours merits special note, as it was entirely a Barrow event. Rail & Coach Tour No. 20 included George Romney's home near Hawcoat Quarry, Furness Abbey, Walney Bridge and Walney Island. To add to the attractions of this tour, Aslett had a Tea Room built at the Romney cottage.

In common with most of the main line railway companies of the period, Aslett extended the variety of cheap tickets. Among the new bookings on the FR were Angler, Golfer and Tennis tickets.

Arguably, Aslett's greatest success was the re-opening of the Barrow-Fleetwood steamer service. This had been closed in 1870, but by 1899 circumstances had totally changed, as Blackpool had now become a thriving holiday resort. There was the prospect of a two-way traffic: from Blackpool via Fleetwood and Barrow to the Circular Tours, and from Barrow and the Furness District to Fleetwood and Blackpool. The FR Board sought tenders for a paddle steamer, and accepted that of J Scott of Kinghorn. The *Lady Evelyn* arrived in Barrow in August 1900 and opened the

Alfred Aslett, *FR General Manager from 1895 to 1918. Starting work on the Great Northern Railway, he became manager of the Eastern & Midlands Railway and General Manager of the Cambrian Railways.*
(From Seaports of the Furness Railway, Geoff Holme collection)

Popular

Sea and Rail Excursions. ::

P.S. "LADY MARGARET."

For further information respecting the Sailings of the Steamers, apply to Mr. F. J. Ramsden, Superintendent of the Line, Barrow; at all Furness Railway Stations; also at any of Messrs. Thos. Cook & Son's Offices; and for conditions under which the tickets are issued, see detailed handbills.

ALFRED ASLETT, *Secretary and General Manager.*

Barrow-in-Furness, March, 1907.

FURNESS RAILWAY.

DAILY (including Sundays) from WHITSUNTIDE until the end of SEPTEMBER,

The Furness Railway Company's Commodious and Fast Paddle Steamers,

"Lady Margaret"

or "Lady Evelyn"

WILL SAIL DAILY (Weather and other unforeseen circumstances permitting) between

Barrow and Fleetwood
(For BLACKPOOL).

Through Return Fares from Barrow to Blackpool
(Fleetwood to Blackpool by Rail)
Saloon and 1st Class, **4/6.**   Fore Cabin and 3rd Class, **2/9.**

FARES—Barrow and Fleetwood:
Saloon—Single, **2/6,**   Return, **3/-,**
Fore Cabin—Single, **1/6,**   Return, **2/-.**

Tickets are also issued between **BARROW & BLACKPOOL**

For Two Days, or from Friday or Saturday to the following Sunday, Monday or Tuesday, as follows:
Saloon and 1st Class, **5/9.**   Fore Cabin and 3rd Class, **3/9.**

Weekly Tickets—Barrow and Fleetwood:
For **SEVEN** Return Journeys—Saloon, **10/-.**   Fore Cabin, **6/-.**

Season Tickets—Barrow and Fleetwood:
Saloon—One Month, **£1 5s.**   Two Months, **£1 12s. 6d.**
For the Season, **£2.**

No Luggage Allowed.

Luncheons, Teas, and Refreshments provided on board by SPIERS & POND, Ltd.

Furness Railway Advertisement.   *(From Mates Guide Book to The Furness Railway 1903, Geoff Holme collection)*

George Romney's Early Home, *c.1910. This cottage at Hawcoat Quarry, home of the famous Dalton born portrait artist from 1742 to 1755, was leased in 1906 by Victor Cavendish of Holker Hall for the Furness Railway. It was turned into a Romney Museum and featured in one of the FR Circular Tours.*   *(H. Bentley, Barrow. Authors collection)*

Barrow - Fleetwood service. In the first full season, 1901, there were 28,000 bookings, and by 1906 these had risen to 120,000. The *Lady Margaret* was added to the fleet in 1903. She was replaced by the *Philomel* in 1908, which in turn was replaced by the *Lady Moyra* in 1910. By the end of 1912 Aslett had increased the number of passenger bookings on the FR by 53% and passenger revenue by 44%.

In the area of operating expenses Aslett was equally successful. The Financial Times of 19th August 1899 noted that the ratio of expenses to receipts was, at 48%, the lowest of the country's railways. It went on: *For the most satisfactory net result and dividend among British railways in the last six months, the palm must be handed to the Furness Company.* It might be thought from the foregoing that in Aslett's early years there were no problems. Nothing could be further from the truth. There were two very serious concerns: the Midland Railway's Heysham Harbour project, and the consequences of the purchase of Barrow shipyard by Vickers Sons and Maxim. The Barrow-Isle of Man and the Barrow-Belfast services dated back to the opening of the Furness and Midland Joint Line between Wennington and Carnforth in 1867. These Barrow routes were not highly profitable, in fact in their early years ran at a loss, but they brought traffic to the two railway companies.

The Midland Railway had obtained an Act for a branch from Morecambe to Heysham in 1892, well before Aslett's appointment. In 1895 the MR deposited a Bill for a harbour at Heysham. Aslett was immediately in contact with MR director G H Turner to convey the FR Board's goodwill towards its partner in the Barrow Route indicating that it did not intend to oppose the Bill. The Heysham scheme was a major engineering project and was not to be completed until 1904. Over these years the Midland's position hardened to one in which they would close the Barrow Route, compensating their partners, the FR and James Little & Co. There were many meetings and various compromises discussed, the FR being led by their Chairman, the 8th Duke of Devonshire.

The Heysham-Belfast service opened on 1st September 1904 and was operated by four brand new steamers. There was a catastrophic fall in Barrow Route receipts, and it was agreed that the Midland Company would purchase the Barrow Steam Navigation Company ships and operate a thrice-weekly service to Belfast. The summer season Isle of Man sailings were to be discontinued at the end of the 1907 season. The beginning of the 1914-18 war and the requisition by the Admiralty of the Barrow-Belfast steamers *City of Belfast* and *Duchess of Devonshire* on 30th October 1914 saw the end of the service.

Apart from ship replacement, there was little capital expenditure on the Barrow and Belfast route. The Shipbuilding Company, however, was to be quite another matter. The original Devonshire and Buccleuch Docks were planned in 1862 to facilitate the rapidly growing coastwise shipping traffic in Furness haematite ore and in pig iron. By the time the Devonshire Dock was completed in 1867, timber importers were operating, and the steelworks, opened in 1864, was exporting rails and other steel products. Much of this traffic was international and used much larger vessels. Even before the Buccleuch Dock was completed in 1872, plans for a much larger dock with a new and deeper dock entrance were before Parliament. This was to be the Ramsden Dock. All of this activity encouraged the formation, in 1873, of the Barrow Shipbuilding Company, whose directors included the Duke of Devonshire, Lord Frederick Cavendish and Sir James Ramsden (Ramsden had been knighted in 1872), all Furness Railway directors. The ships constructed, although being large for their day, were well within the capacity of the Barrow Dock cills. The new dock opened in 1879. The Barrow Shipbuilding Company had mixed fortunes, and was reconstituted in 1888 as Naval Construction and Armaments Ltd., presaging a change of emphasis at the Barrow yard toward warships.

Buccleuch Dock Bridge, *1908. The ever increasing size of naval vessels being built by Vickers' Barrow Shipyard necessitated the widening of the passageway between the Buccleuch and Ramsden Docks to 100 feet. In connection with this work a new bascule bridge of Scherzer type replaced the original two-span swing bridge. The new bridge, seen under construction, was opened for traffic in October 1908. It carried a road and interlaced rail tracks. It was demolished in about 1972.* (Wyn Anderson collection)

In 1897 two armaments manufacturers, Vickers of Sheffield and Maxim of Crayford in SE London, combined and became known as Vickers, Sons and Maxim. Before the year was out, they had snapped up the Barrow shipyard and embarked on a ruthless campaign to dominate UK warship production. The battleship *HMS Vengeance*, launched on 25th July 1899 was the first to be built, armoured and supplied with gun mountings by one firm. The 1st Class Cruiser *HMS Powerful* had been successfully undocked by NC&A in 1896, but *HMS Vengeance* was another matter. Vickers wrote to the FR on 8th February 1899 on the subject of the Ramsden Dock gates: *The matter is of considerable importance in view of the ever increasing size of ships and for the little margin of room for the battleship now being built by our firm for the Imperial Japanese Government* (Mikasa). *The condition of your dock cills will, as you are aware, make it necessary for us to send the ship into the open in an incomplete condition . . .*

The FR had to agree to the lowering of the Ramsden Dock No. 4 cill at a cost of £85,000, of which Vickers agreed to pay half. It was also agreed that the work would be completed in time for *HMS Vengeance* to undock. It was not a happy story. A subsidence seriously delayed the work and incurred a letter from Vickers to the FR in December 1900:

The state of the works have caused the Government, in spite of all our endeavours, to refuse to allow us to tender for the last four cruisers given to the trade. Until the cill is completed we are not in position to deliver the battleship Vengeance which has been waiting delivery since July last, nor to complete the cruiser Hogue or the battleship Mikasa . . . we will look to you to recoup the very heavy losses we are daily sustaining from the neglect of the Railway Company to finish the lowering of the cill.

The work was completed and *HMS Vengeance* was undocked in May 1901.

The dispute between Vickers and the FR over clearances in Barrow Docks lingered on, and concerned the passage between the Buccleuch and Ramsden Docks, the dredging of a deep-water berth in Walney Channel between the Belfast Pier and the Harbour yard, and Piel Bar. Regarding the Buccleuch Dock passage, Vickers demanded that the opening be increased from 80 to 100 feet at FR expense, otherwise they would transfer the building of Atlantic liners to the Beardmore Yard on the Clyde (in which they had a half share). The FR had to agree and a tender was let for £38,422.

Commissioned on 12th October 1908 the Buccleuch Dock Bascule Bridge carried an interlaced pair of railway tracks and a roadway. These items of expenditure did little for FR receipts and added to the FR's Capital Account burden. In 1910 the FR and Barrow Corporation considered the possibility of a jointly owned 'Barrow Docks and Harbour Trust' based on the model of the Mersey Docks and Harbour Board. Concern was expressed by veteran FR Board member Edward Wadham on the dangers of the FR losing control of the docks, and the scheme was dropped. Aslett wrote to Vickers in November 1912:

We are at all times desirous of meeting you in the most liberal manner and in every possible way so far as we can reasonably be asked or expected to do. There must however come a time when we cannot go on spending money on dredging work, as far as our Capital Account is concerned, unless we can see a fair and proper return for this outlay and which, when incurred, it must be remembered will necessarily involve further expenses year by year in maintenance.

Vickers pressure prevailed. On 14th February 1913 the FR Chairman, Victor Cavendish, 9th Duke of Devonshire, told a meeting of shareholders that a deep water berth in Walney Channel had been finished, and that the improvement in the fairway of Walney Channel and Piel Bar would be completed by the end of March. A year later he was able to report that the completion of

Buccleuch Dock Bridge, *7th July 1954, with a workmen's train from Barrow Shipyard station hauled by 2-6-2 tank No. 41221. Note the interlaced tracks to provide space for a roadway.*

(Author MAC 49)

Barrow-in-Furness, Walney Ferry

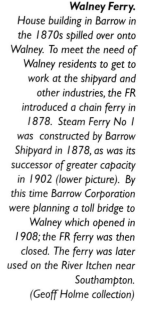

Walney Ferry.
*House building in Barrow in the 1870s spilled over onto Walney. To meet the need of Walney residents to get to work at the shipyard and other industries, the FR introduced a chain ferry in 1878. Steam Ferry No 1 was constructed by Barrow Shipyard in 1878, as was its successor of greater capacity in 1902 (lower picture). By this time Barrow Corporation were planning a toll bridge to Walney which opened in 1908; the FR ferry was then closed. The ferry was later used on the River Itchen near Southampton.
(Geoff Holme collection)*

Walney Ferry

these works *will now enable the largest battleships and battle cruisers to pass safely in and out of Barrow Docks.*

In just a few years from the Vickers' purchase of Barrow shipyard in 1897, the number employed there doubled from 5,000 to 10,000 and there was a shortage of skilled men and of accommodation, similar to that of the early 1870s. In March 1899 Vickers proposed that workmen's trains be run from Ulverston and Dalton to *a point in proximity to the Works.* The FR constructed a platform on the line which crossed Barrow Island. Adjacent to Shipyard Junction, Barrow Shipyard station was opened on 1st May 1899.

The earlier expansion of Barrow industry had led to some small amount of housing development on Walney Island. With its sandy beaches it was also becoming a recreational facility for Barrow's congested population. Access to Walney was by a ford at low water or by rowing boats at other states of the tide. In 1877 the FR announced its intention to provide a steam ferry. Barrow Shipbuilding Company's 'Yard No. 53' was 'Steam Ferry No. 1'. On 1st July 1878 Henry Cook, the FR Secretary and Traffic Manager, formally opened the service.

On 23rd April 1897, before the Vickers purchase of Barrow Shipyard, the FR Board had received a deputation from Barrow Corporation, which proposed that a bridge be built between Old Barrow Island and Walney. The plan was for a bridge south of the ferry and of the Devonshire Dock entrance, and the estimated cost was £40,000. Such a bridge would allow the Barrow tramway system to be extended to Walney. Although the FR ferry had made a loss of £13 in 1896, the FR declined to entertain the plan, principally as it would obstruct access to the Devonshire Dock. On 29th December 1897, the FR Board met Walney landowners who were suggesting a light railway from Ormsgill to Walney; the matter was deferred. By 1899, with Vickers expansion of the shipyard activities, the matter of access to Walney had become more urgent, as Vickers proposed to build a thousand homes on Walney for their workmen and their families. The Walney Estate Company again raised the Walney Bridge & Light Railway scheme, but again the FR declined to support it. Their solution was the provision of a new larger ferry. This was built by Vickers and brought into operation in 1902, providing a 15-minute service. By 1904 Vickers had built 950 homes on their Vickerstown estate and Barrow Corporation obtained an Act in that year for a bridge. The Walney Toll Bridge was formally opened on 18th August 1908.

The Barrow-in-Furness Tramway Co. Ltd. had opened their first line on 11th July 1885 using steam traction, and in 1903 a Tramway Order authorised electrification of the system and for its extension to the Walney Ferry. The new electric trams, operated by the British Electric Traction Co., started on some routes on 6th February 1904, the extension to Walney Ferry being opened later. The latter ran along Ferry Road on the east side of the Furness Railway's Barrow Island line. On the opening of the Walney Bridge, the tramway was moved to the west side of the railway, running along what was now Bridge Road. It was opened in June 1909 to Walney Promenade and to Biggar Bank on 4th August 1911.

The railways of the UK came under Government control at midnight on 4th/5th August 1914 on the outbreak of the 1914-18 war. While it had been popularly assumed that the war would be over by Christmas, it soon became clear that a long campaign was likely. The demands of the Western Front and of the Royal Navy put a great strain on the UK armaments industry generally and Vickers and the Barrow Haematite Steel Co. in particular. As well as their programme of construction of warships and submarines, Vickers embarked on artillery shell manufacture. To keep the Vickers yard and the steelworks supplied with raw materials required a prodigious effort by the Furness Railway. Notable in this context was the importation of iron ore through Barrow Docks for onward carriage to the iron and steel works of Furness and South and West Cumberland.

Government Control had broken down the traditional barriers between railway companies, and, as the war effort increased and the FR locomotive and wagon fleet came under increasing strain, LNWR and Maryport & Carlisle locomotives began to appear on the FR system. The numbers employed by Vickers grew steadily, and workers had to be drawn from an ever increasing distance; this required a major expansion of the shipyard workmen's trains. On 18th October 1915 a second platform was brought into use at Shipyard Station. Some idea of the size of this traffic is given by the figures for the first 12 weeks of 1916 and 1917:
1916 - Ordinary passengers 558,385 Workmen 769,755
1917 - do. 379,378 do. 771,552

Early in 1918 there seemed to be no prospect of an early end to the war and Alfred Aslett, now aged 71, resigned and was replaced by Lionel Speakman of the LNWR Goods Department, Manchester.

Although the war ended in November 1918, Government Control continued until 15th August 1921. In the same month the Railways Act required that the existing railway companies be amalgamated into four groups with effect from 1st January 1923.

In August 1922 an attempt was made to revive the Barrow-Fleetwood steamer service. The chartered steamer *Robina* ran from 12th August to 22nd September, but there was a loss of £73 and the service was never resumed.

Another interesting post-war experiment was a shuttle service between a newly constructed halt platform on the Piel Branch near Salthouse Junction and Piel station. This operated on Saturdays only and started on 22nd May 1920. A modified service with trains from Piel

Barrow Trams, *c. 1900. Barrow's tramway system opened in 1885 with steam traction. The steam engines were built by Kitson and the trailers were built by Brush. Electric traction took over in 1904. The system served the FR stations at Barrow Central, Barrow Ramsden Dock, Walney Ferry, Roose and Furness Abbey. A steam tram and trailer in Duke Street passes the corner of Cavendish Street with a full load in the last days before the system was closed for conversion to electic power.* (*Geoff Holme collection*)

Furness Abbey Station. *On 21st May 1915, the Royal train is hauled by immaculate 4-4-0s Nos.132 and 133. From Furness Abbey the Royal party was taken to Vickers works by motor car.* (H. Bentley, Barrow, Geoff Holme collection)

running alternatively to the halt and to Barrow Central was tried in the summer of 1921, thereafter being discontinued as unsuccessful.

From 1890 the production of iron ore in Furness started to dwindle as the mines were progressively worked out, and the needs of the blast furnaces at Barrow, Askam, Millom and Ulverston had increasingly to be met by importing ore through Barrow Docks. Some 45,500 tons were imported in 1899 and the unloading into wagons was carried out largely on the north and south side of the Ramsden Dock basin. The original rail line from South Side made a west-facing junction with the main Dock line at Buccleuch Bridge Junction. This resulted in train loads of ore to the Barrow Haematite Works at Hindpool having to reverse twice,

Furness Abbey Hotel, *showing the lavishly furnished drawing room.* (Green Brothers, Grasmere Geoff Holme collection)

VISIT OF PRINCE FUSHIMI TO BARROW
APPROACHING THE SHIPYARD

Island Road, *21st May 1907. The line through Shipyard Junction to Island Road was used over the years for special trains carrying VIPs to Vickers Works. FR 4-4-0, No. 128 built in 1901, suitably decorated, with Furness Railway No 1 saloon behind, passes St John's Church with a train carrying Prince Fushimi. The Shipyard was building the battleship* Kongo *for the Imperial Japanese Navy at this time.* (Lance Kelly collection)

occupying the single line on the Buccleuch Bridge and involving a propelling movement back through Loco Junction. To improve the working, a new east-facing junction for the South Side was made at Loco Junction. This new curve was opened on 1st September 1901 and the original curve closed.

Matters were improved even further in 1903 when a loop from Loco Junction to Salthouse Junction, using part of the siding to Claye's rolling stock works, allowed the engines of ore trains to Hindpool to run round their train. This eliminated propelling movements altogether.

Salthouse Halt, *April 1955. This was opened in May 1920 for a Summer Saturdays only shuttle service to Piel. It was not a success and was discontinued a year later. In the background is Barrow Gasworks.* (Author MAC 24)

Top
Island Road, *site of the future Shipyard Station, c.1875, an early view looking south. This was the line which connected Shipyard Junction with Walney Ferry and Barrow Yard and served the shipyard. The buildings on the right are thought to be a Sunday School and the Old Barrow Arms.*
(George Taylor collection)

Middle
Shipyard Junction, 1963. *The signalbox dates from 1912. In the foreground are the two platforms of Barrow Shipyard station used by workmen's trains and the occasional excursion. An earlier station on this site was opened in 1899.*
(Author MAA 30)

Bottom
Shipyard Station looking north, *1963. The evening trains for Grange (left) and Silecroft (right) are ready to depart.*
(Author MAA 33)

There had been line closures in the Barrow area during the Furness Railway era, notably two sections of the original line of 1846. The transfer of the Isle of Man and Belfast steamers from Piel Pier to Ramsden Dock rendered the section between Roose Junction and Parrock Hall redundant, and it closed on 27th March 1882. After the opening of the through route via Barrow Central in 1882, the only traffic between Goldmire Junction and Millwood Junction was a train that ran between Coniston and Furness Abbey, presumably to serve the FR's Furness Abbey Hotel. This did not last long after the through line was opened, and the section was closed on 12th December 1898.

The Park Loop, opened in 1882, included a curve between Oak Lea Junction and Goldmire Junction. This was intended to provide a direct route between Stainton Quarry and the Barrow Haematite Steel Company works at Hindpool for limestone traffic. It does not appear to have been used regularly for very long, being shown as 'closed' in the FR Appendix to the Working Timetable of 1899. The curve was officially closed on 4th December 1908. Interestingly, only the points were removed at Millwood, Goldmire and Oak Lea Junctions, the track being left to maintain the railway 'right of way'. It was however taken up in the 1914-18 war to provide material for additional sidings in Barrow. Goldmire Junction remained on an 'open as required' basis, as it controlled the siding into the Goldmire Quarry of the Millom & Askam Haematite Iron Company. Later this was replaced by a ground frame controlled by Annetts key kept at Park South signal box.

The branch from Salthouse Junction to Stank Mine, opened in 1873, was closed beyond Fishers Sand Wharf at Roose in 1901 as a result of the mine being worked out. This closure allowed a new Rampside road to be built in the early 1920s.

On 1st January 1923, the Furness Railway, LNWR and the Midland Railway, together with numerous other lines, became part of the London, Midland & Scottish Railway. The LMS inherited the workshops of its large number of constituents. It was inevitable that rationalisation would be necessary, and in England work was gradually concentrated on the LNWR's Crewe Works, the Midland Railway's Derby Works and the Lancashire & Yorkshire Railway's Horwich Works. However, possibly because of its remoteness, the FR's Barrow Works survived until 1931. Thereafter locomotives from the FR Section were sent to Horwich, and some of the FR 0-6-0s were reboilered with L&Y boilers. Private firms occupied some parts of the Barrow Works, for example the North West Wagon Company, until rail access was removed in the 1970s.

When the Park Loop opened in 1882 there was a considerable traffic in iron ore between Park Mine and Barrow Ironworks. Ormsgill Junction controlled the branch into the ironworks. Connections from the up and down goods lines into other local works were controlled by a separate signal box nearer to Barrow Central; Cocken Junction signalled the goods lines only. The output of Park Mine began to drop after 1900, and Barrow Ironworks became increasingly reliant on foreign ore imported through Barrow Docks. Ormsgill Junction was closed on 12th December 1935, and Cocken Junction on 6th July 1936.

After the failure of the *Robina* service to Fleetwood in 1922, Ramsden Dock Station had no regular passenger traffic, though there were occasional cruises and excursions. Dockyard Junction and Dock Station signalboxes were closed on 8th December 1936, and the station demolished soon after. By 1937 the Barrow Shipyard was again busy, and 1939 saw the beginning of another war effort by Vickers and the Barrow Haematite Steel Company.

Walney Ferry, c.1963. In the foreground is the gate which was closed to the road when a train was passing. The iron and steel works are in the distance. The line to the right leads to Bridge Road sidings and to the left into the North West yard of Vickers works. (Author MAA 42)

Shipyard Junction, *7th July 1954. 4F 0-6-0 No. 44368 heads for Loco Junction with an evening workmen's train for Silecroft. On the left a FR signal protects the trailing junction from the oil depot.*　　　　　　　　　　　　　　　　*(Author MAC 53)*

Barrow was heavily bombed in April/May 1941, the Central Station being seriously damaged on the night of 6th-7th May. The large roof had to be taken down, and bare platforms sufficed until the rebuilding of 'Barrow-in-Furness' station in 1958-9. At the end of the war in 1945, the 'Big Four' railway companies were physically and financially exhausted, and the Labour Government saw nationalisation as the only solution. British Railways came into being on 1st January 1948 as part of the British Transport Commission.

Barrow had two 'suburban' stations on the main line, those at Furness Abbey and Roose. Roose was well patronised from local housing estates and continues to be so. Furness Abbey was different. It had the LMS Hotel, the nearby Abbey ruins and the prestigious Abbey House designed by Lutyens and built in 1914 for the accommodation and entertainment of Vickers clients. To the east was Abbots Wood, still occupied, until his death in 1941, by Frederick Ramsden, Sir James' only son, a former FR Director and Chairman. These did not provide much traffic.

Roose Station, *c. 1966. Two Derby Lightweight DMUs form an Up stopping train for Carnforth and Lancaster.　(Author　MAO 2810)*

Barrow Central.

Top: The severe damage caused by a bomb on the night of 6/7th May 1941. The overall roof had to be dismantled.   (Dock Museum, Barrow)

Middle: A view of the bare platforms which served from 1941 to 1958.   (Ken Norman collection)

Bottom: When the station rebuilding was completed in 1958 the name 'Central' was dropped.   (J Martin Hurst, Ken Norman collection)

Furness Abbey, *1956. In connection with the relining of the tunnel in 1956-9, the up and down lines were interlaced and operated as a single line. To control this a signalbox was constructed on the down platform. On the right is the vehicle used for tunnel work.* (Author MAA 4)

After the war the hotel never reopened and was demolished, with the exception of the public house and restaurant named Abbey Tavern. In spite of this, Furness Abbey had a good train service. In the summer timetable of 1948, as well as the local stopping trains, the 10.40 Euston to Barrow and the 17.45 Liverpool Exchange to Whitehaven down trains and the 06.30 Workington to Euston and the 10.05 Workington to Preston up trains all called. On Saturdays the 10.00 Bolton Trinity Street to Barrow via Hellifield and the 10.35 Leeds to Barrow stopped at Furness Abbey. The up bay, the down loop and the signal box had closed on 29th March 1936, and, hardly surprisingly, the station itself closed on 25th September 1950. There was a flurry of activity at Furness Abbey in 1956-59 during the relining of the tunnel. A temporary signal box was built on the down platform, which by then had lost its buildings. This box was to control, by single line working, the interlaced track through the tunnel.

The closure of lines and signal boxes in the Barrow area up to the 1950s did not significantly reduce the railway system. The main impact of the Beeching Report was the rationalisation of freight services and the closure of many private sidings which had handled wagonload traffic. This was a process that had already started, due to the increasing competition from road vehicles with their greater flexibility. The branch to the Yarlside Mine from Roose closed in 1956. The almost total destruction of Barrow's railway system could be seen to start in 1966 and was associated with the decline of traffic through Barrow Docks, hived off from British Railways to the British Transport Docks Board in 1963. Matters were brought to a head by an engineers' report on the condition of the Buccleuch Dock rolling and lifting Scherzer bridge. Because of the deterioration of the contact surfaces, and the lack of justification of the cost of repair because of the greatly reduced traffic, it was decided that the bridge would remain open to shipping traffic and

Barrow-in-Furness station *looking south, 22nd October 1970. Barrow-in-Furness South box beyond Abbey Road Bridge had closed on 24th May, platform 4 had its' line removed and platform 3 terminated in buffer-stops, thereafter only being used for trains to and from the north. South box, which replaced the original FR structure on 1st July 1928, was a LNWR style box with a LNWR frame and instruments.* (Author MAA 810)

Ramsden Dock Basin, 16th August 1950. Barrow coal engine No. 28166 poses in the sidings serving the north side. (Ian Pearsall V69)

closed to rail traffic from 1st January 1967. This would mean that the line to Ramsden Dock North Side and to the Shipyard Station would have to close. To allow for the possibility of some new traffic at the docks, it was agreed that the bridge and the signal box at Shipyard Junction would be put into a 'care and maintenance' status. There was the problem that the statutory passenger train closure procedure had to be followed, and it seems that the workmen's trains continued until 3rd July 1967 when they were replaced by buses between Barrow Central (now renamed Barrow-in-Furness) and the shipyard. The replacement bus service was discontinued from 7th October 1968. As there seemed to be no prospect of new docks traffic, Shipyard Junction and Island Road signal boxes were finally closed on 14th December 1969. At the same time Buccleuch Dock Bridge was permanently taken out of use and subsequently dismantled. This allowed the passageway between the Buccleuch and Ramsden Docks to be widened.

By this time the reduction in wagonload traffic led to the decision that the extensive sidings along the east side of the Buccleuch and Devonshire Docks, the Barrow Yard, were significantly in excess of requirements. Early in 1970, Barrow Yard was transferred to the sidings between Salthouse and Loco junctions, and the old yard taken up with the exception of a single line to the Vickers works and the remaining part of the steelworks, Barrow ironworks having closed in 1963. Traffic through Loco Junction was now very small and it was closed on 31st August 1970. St Luke's Junction now controlled access to the running shed. The two single lines to Vickers and the steelworks and to Ramsden Dock South Side were controlled by Salthouse Junction. The steelworks line was closed on 18th September 1973 to allow the bridge over North Road to be demolished in connection with a road improvement scheme. Access to the steelworks was then by a siding at Ormsgill operated by a ground frame.

Buccleuch Dock Bridge from Shipyard Junction, 2nd August 1952. Notice the slewing of tracks for the re-building in 1908. Barrow coal engine No. 28293 runs tender first towards North Side sidings. On the left is the siding to the west side of Buccleuch Dock formerly serving Crossfields timber yard. (Ian Pearsall C859)

93

Barrow Ironworks.
The slag ladle was used to take waste slag from the furnaces to the top of the bank, illustrated opposite. At night, when the slag was tipped, it lit up the night sky. (Derek Walmsley collection)

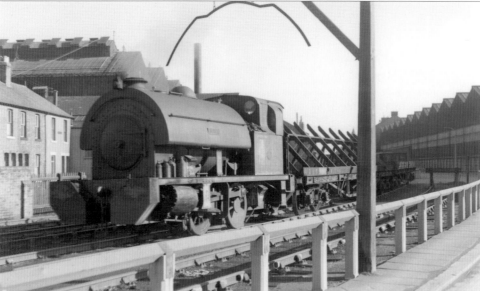

Bridge Road Sidings,
c.1960. The Vickers locomotives regularly shunted in these sidings. 0-4-0 saddle tank Jupiter built by Robert Stephenson & Hawthorn, Newcastle in 1943, on a train. (Author MAA 41/1)

Crow Nest, *10th September 1964. Looking along Ferry Road (left) and Bridge Road (right) towards Michaelson Road. Centre right is a transit shed with its own siding, and the siding curving to the left ran alongside Stanley Road to Barrow shipyard.* (Author MAT A35)

Top
Hindpool North,
March 1955.
This box, dating from 1890, controlled the north end of the iron and steelworks sidings. In the distance an ironworks loco propels a slag hopper to the top of the slag bank.
(Author MAC 77)

Middle
Barrow Yard looking south from the High Level Bridge at the time of closure, 30th August 1970.
(Author MAA 777)

Barrow Loco Shed, 3rd June 1971. This large running shed dated from 1874. Behind the class 40 diesel locomotive can be seen the roof damaged by fire in the mid 1960s and never repaired. The shed closed in 1977 and was soon demolished.   (Author MAA 845)

Ward's scrapyard south of Cornmill Crossing, c.1989, with a Class 47 locomotive on the Barrow trip train. These lines finally closed in 1990.
(Jaye Hartley)

On 16th December 1973, St Luke's Junction was closed and access to Barrow running shed was by a direct line from Salthouse Junction. The running shed finally closed in 1977 and fuelling facilities were concentrated at Barrow station carriage sidings. Vickers, by now Vickers Shipbuilding & Engineering Ltd. (VSEL), obtained a Light Railway Order in June 1986 for the single line from Barrow Goods to their works entrance in Stanley Road. However the last train ran during the early hours of Sunday, 14th December 1986. The line then fell into disuse and was taken up by 1990, except for a short section opposite the Dock Museum. The north end of the Devonshire Dock is now occupied by the Devonshire Dock Hall, allowing construction of submarines and large parts of surface vessels under cover.

A coal concentration depot was opened at Cart Sidings by E Holme, a Barrow coal merchant, in 1964, rail traffic to which ceased in late 1986. The final trip train to Ward's scrap yard adjacent to Cornmill Crossing was on 30th June 1989, and the following day the line from Loco Junction to Walney Ferry was formally closed. Track lifting of the section from Loco Junction to Cornmill Crossing took place during December 1990.

This left Salthouse Junction as solely concerned with the single line to Ramsden Dock South Side, which carried the traffic to the British Nuclear Fuels terminal. Salthouse Junction was closed and replaced by a ground frame on 6th September 1992. Dalton Junction, Barrow-in-Furness and Park South signal boxes now control the line through Barrow.

Ramsden Dock, c.1989. Class 31 diesel locomotive bearing the Freight Sector logo stands at the British Nuclear Fuels facility with a train of flasks.
(Jaye Hartley)

Chapter 17: The Future

Those who remember Barrow's rail system prior to 1967 may think that it has virtually been destroyed. In terms of track mileage this is so, but it must be recognised that the core railway, the main line from Carnforth through Barrow to Whitehaven, Workington and Carlisle remains intact, and there still is a rail line into Barrow Docks used by the nuclear flask trains, operated by Direct Rail Services based in Carlisle, with space available for other traffic to be handled. The Ramsden Dock gate has again been enlarged and Barrow Shipyard, under yet another owner, BAE Systems, continues Barrow's shipbuilding tradition, with surface vessels being built on the old slipways for launch into Walney Channel. However, following the launch of Landing Platform Dock vessels *Albion* and *Bulwark* in 2000 & 2001, the berths are again empty and face an uncertain future. The Barrow yard has been designated as a submarine centre of excellence, this work being carried out in the Devonshire Dock Hall complex, without the need for traditional dynamic launches into Walney Channel.

After years of under use of the remaining derelict parts of the docks estate south of St George's Square, proposals are being developed for a light industrial estate and marina centred on Ramsden and Cavendish Docks.

Train Operating Company 'First North Western' operates a frequent express service between Manchester Airport and Barrow, in addition to stopping trains, some of which run between Lancaster and Carlisle via Barrow. These services provide connections into both Virgin West Coast trains and the Virgin CrossCountry routes to Brighton, Poole and Penzance. A new class of DMU, the Class 175, has appeared on the Barrow-Manchester Airport service, and Virgin is introducing new tilting trains for the West Coast Main Line London to Glasgow services. The line is currently undergoing a major refurbishment and re-signalling to increase the maximum permissible speed to 125 m.p.h. New Voyager diesel trains are already in service on cross-country routes.

The signalling between Carnforth and West Cumberland still utilises manual frame boxes, some of which date from the 19th century, and there are numerous manned level crossings. The plans of the track owner and signalling operator, Network Rail, are less well developed, activity being concentrated on the re-signalling of the West Coast Main Line.

New Rail Franchise agreements are at present being negotiated, which will see the Barrow to Manchester Airport service being incorporated into a Trans-Pennine service. The remaining local services are to become part of a new Northern England franchise. First Group/Keolis have been awarded the TransPennine franchise and are expected to commence operations early in 2004. A number of operators, including First Group, are bidding for the remaining local services franchise and a decision on the future shape of the passenger service is expected shortly with changes due to take effect in 2004.

All in all, at the start of the new Millennium, the prospects for Barrow's remaining railway seem brighter than they have for many years.

To conclude is a series of photographs of the current railway scene and showing new uses for former railway land.

Barrow Central, May 2001. The new and the old - a new Class 175 'Coradia' unit passes the Furness Railway built Barrow-in-Furness (formerly Barrow Central North) signalbox first opened in July 1907, all trains still being signalled by the original, now unique, mechanical frame manufactured by F W Atkinson, London.

(Geoff Holme GH 546.4.2)

Devonshire Dock Hall and Dock Museum,
4th May 2000.
Outside the Devonshire Dock Hall, built on the site of the filled-in Devonshire Dock basin, is a section of the hull of Albion, *built inside the hall and transported by road to the slipways of Walney Channel for final assembly and launch. To the right the Dock Museum makes good use of the former Graving Dock, and beyond is the filled-in Devonshire Dock entrance basin. A busy road has replaced the road-rail bridge seen on page 46.*
(Geoff Holme GH 542.6.1)

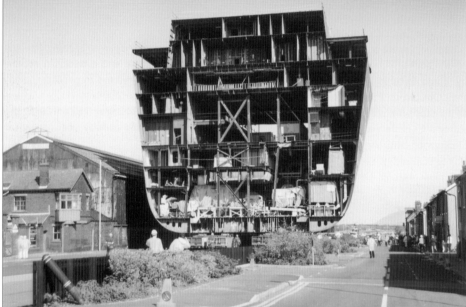

Bridge Road, *4th May 2000. The tracks seen on page 94 have long been taken up and the Vickers internal railway system closed. Car parks have now been built on the site. Bridge Road has been rebuilt and strengthened to allow loads in excess of 2000 tons to be taken from the Devonshire Dock Hall by road back to the slipways alongside Walney Channel for final assembly and launch. Here the largest section of* Albion *is being taken from the Devonshire Dock Hall to the slipways. At the time it was the heaviest load to have ever been carried on a public highway in Britain.*
(Geoff Holme GH 542.8.1)

Buccleuch Dock, *10th June 2003. Excursions by sea returned to Barrow for one day on 11th June 2003 when the* Balmoral, *built 1949, ran a trip from Belfast Quay on the site of Ramsden Dock station to Douglas, Isle of Man. Here the vessel is seen the night before alongside the new quay by Morrisons Supermarket, only opened the previous day. This Supermarket has replaced all the sidings and railway buildings from the High Level Bridge as far as the old station at St George's Square. Compare this scene with the busy marshalling yard on page 95.*
(Geoff Holme)

Dalton Junction, 10th April 2003. English, Welsh & Scottish Railways class 66 No. 66169 in charge of a train of new rails rolled at the Corus plant at Workington approaches Dalton Junction from Park South, avoiding the need for the lengthy detour round Barrow. The signal on the left acts as a Starting signal for Dalton Junction and a Distant signal from Park South for northbound trains. (Alan Johnstone AJ-03-4982)

Dalton, 3rd August 2001. 'Northern Belle' excursion passes through hauled by 47798 Prince William. Luxury train operators VSOE have in recent years run a number of excursions from either Liverpool or Manchester Victoria to Barrow where lunch or dinner is served on the train. (Alan Johnstone AJ-01-0385)

Barrow station, 7th July 2003. Direct Rail Services class 37 diesel No. 37218 in charge of a train carrying nuclear material from Barrow Docks to Sellafield for re-processing. (Alan Johnstone AJ-03-5582)

Roose, *4th July 2003. The station buildings were all swept away following the withdrawal of staff in the late 1960s, and the new Class 175 unit 175 109 is seen here passing through Roose bound for Manchester Airport. The station remains and serves an area where most of the factories have been closed and demolished and additional housing is being built on the sites and the nearby Holbeck estate.*
(Alan Johnstone AJ-03-5572)

Barrow, *17th October 2002, the station carriage sidings from Devonshire Road Bridge. Although the sidings layout remains largely intact a fuelling point was built in the late 1970s following the final closure of Barrow shed in 1977. The carriage storage sheds seen in the photographs on pages 67 and 69 have long been demolished and storage is now in the open. Stock is still stabled, cleaned and prepared here overnight for the following day's duties when most of the sidings are used. Here a First North Western Class 153 No. 153 367 heads north onto the single line to Park South with the 14.58 train to Carlisle.* *(Alan Johnstone AJ-02-4071)*

Index

ACKNOWLEDGMENTS

The writer wishes to thank the following for providing assistance with the research for this book:

The Clerk of the Records, House of Lords Record Office for Parliamentary Acts, bills, deposited plans and proceedings of committees on bills.

The Keeper of the Records, Public Record Office, Kew for the records of the Furness Railway Company and of the Board of Trade Railway Department.

The Director of the British Library for maps and plans and files of local newspapers.

Area Archivist, Barrow Record Office for use of the local collection including the Kendall Collection and the microfilm copy of the Diary of 7th Duke of Devonshire.

Over many years a number of individuals have given the writer assistance with his project. While it is not possible to name them all, particular thanks must go to Dr Edwin Course, formerly of London University, who put the writer on the right track in 1954, the late John Campbell (an ex Maryport and Carlisle railwayman) who revealed the treasures of the British Transport Historical Records at 66 Porchester Road, London and the late Edward Telford of the LMR District Engineer's Office, Barrow who opened up his historical files.

In more recent times Geoffrey Holme of Barrow has made a significant input to the text in relation to the great changes in Barrow's railway system in the last 35 years, and has carried out invaluable photographic work in connection with the illustrations. His associate Alan Johnstone has used his computing skills to draw maps and plans and to set out the book for publishing, and Phil Cousins of PR Design has prepared the cover.

Finally, Ken Norman of Barrow, veteran writer on the Furness Railway, and Alan Pearsall, maritime and railway historian, formerly of the National Maritime Museum, have read the manuscript and made valuable suggestions. Ken Norman has prepared the index.

Any errors or omissions are the responsibility of the author.

BIBLIOGRAPHY

F Barnes: *Barrow and District, an illustrated history* (Barrow Corporation, 1967)

D Joy: *Regional History of the Railways of Great Britain Volume 14, The Lake Counties* (David and Charles, 1983)

F Leach: *Barrow-in-Furness, Its rise and development* (Barrow-in-Furness, 1872)

J D Marshall: *Furness and the Industrial Revolution* (Barrow-in-Furness Library and Museum Committee, 1958)

K J Norman: *Furness Railway* (Silver Link Publishing, Kettering, 2001)

B Trescatheric: *Building Barrow* (Barrow-in-Furness, 1992)

Back Cover

Top
Buccleuch Dock from the large crane beside Devonshire Dock, c. 1959. The aircraft carrier Hermes is at the Buccleuch Dock fitting out birth. The High Level bridge in the foreground was built in two sections and here one section is 'raised' for maintenance clear of the 80ft. channel connecting Buccleuch and Devonshire Docks. Cavendish Dock and Roose power station are shown in the background. (Ken Norman)

Centre
Coat of Arms of the Borough of Barrow in Furness.
Piel to Barrow Single ticket.
Circular tour ticket issued at Roose.
Tour ticket issued at Furness Abbey.
Douglas to Ambleside return issued at Douglas for use via Piel Pier (before Ramsden Dock station was built) by the Barrow Steam Navigation Company.

Bottom
Barrow Central Station, c. 1964. Metrovick Co-Bo No. D5710 awaits its next turn of duty in the former Piel Bay at the south end of Barrow station. This class of 20 locomotives, drafted into Furness around 1962, were one of the least successful designs of the 1950s British Railways modernisation plan and had all gone by early 1968, before the steam engines they were built to replace. The cooling tower of the former Corporation power station in Buccleuch Street can be seen behind Abbey Road railway bridge. (Wyn Anderson WH848)